Praise for *You Don't Sweat Much for a Fat Girl*

"Rivenbark's as rebellious, irreverent, and comical as ever."

—*Publishers Weekly*

"A rip-roaring read . . . What makes Rivenbark's writing so entertaining is that it's a lot like seeing a stand-up comedy act; she does an uncanny job of keeping the flow of comedy fresh."

—*Book Reporter*

"Opening a book by Celia is like going to a great party—at the end of the night, your sides hurt, your mascara's ruined, and you realize you haven't eaten anything for almost an hour. She's *that* good. My biggest hope is that when I find myself riding the bus to hell, I'll look over and Celia will be sitting right next to me."

—Laurie Notaro, author of *The Idiot Girls' Action-Adventure Club*

Praise for *You Can't Drink All Day If You Don't Start in the Morning*

"Whether readers are from the South Side of Baw-ston or living just south of the Mississippi, Rivenbark's genuine Southern recipes and true Southern charm are sure to appeal to everyone."

—*Encore Archives*

"Many of her descriptions are not only LOL funny, they also demand reading aloud to whoever happens to be nearby."

—*Myrtle Beach Sun-News*

"Rivenbark is more than funny, she's Carolina funny."

—*The Charlotte Observer*

Praise for *Belle Weather*

"Readers will laugh out loud over her commentary on status mothers and all the odd obsessions of modern life."   —*Booklist*

"Think Dave Barry with a female point of view. . . ."   —*USA Today*

Praise for *Stop Dressing Your Six-Year-Old Like a Skank*

"This is a hilarious read, perhaps best enjoyed while eating Krispy Kreme doughnuts with a few girlfriends."   —*Publishers Weekly*

"She kills in the 'Kids' and 'Southern-Style Silliness' sections, putting the fear of Mickey into anyone planning a trip to Disney World (character breakfasts must be scheduled ninety days in advance) and extolling the entertainment value of obituaries ('If there's a nickname in quotes, say Red Eye, Tip Top, or simply, Zeke, then my entire day is made')."

—*Entertainment Weekly*

Praise for *We're Just Like You, Only Prettier*

"Will give you a case of the giggles."   —*NY Daily News*

"Warm, witty, and wise, rather like reading dispatches from a friend who uses e-mail but still writes letters, in ink, on good paper."

—*St. Petersburg Times*

Praise for *Bless Your Heart, Tramp*

"Bright, witty, and warm . . . stories that make a desperate gift-giver weep glad tears of relief . . . A pleasing blend of spice, humor, and memories."

—*St. Petersburg Times*

"Celia Rivenbark has the goods and then some. She makes you laugh out loud dozens of times. Anyone who has the moxie to toss off a piece titled 'Fake Dog Testicles' will tread into the wildest stretches of comedic terrain."   —*The State* (Columbia, S.C.)

Celia Rivenbark

✳

rude bitches make me tired

✳

slightly profane and
entirely logical answers
to modern etiquette
dilemmas

St. Martin's Griffin
New York

www.stmartins.com

Design by Kathryn Parise

THE LIBRARY OF CONGRESS CATALOGING-IN-PUBLICATION DATA
IS AVAILABLE UPON REQUEST

ISBN 978-1-250-02923-2 (trade paperback)
ISBN 978-1-250-03841-8 (e-book)

First Edition: October 2013

10 9 8 7 6 5 4 3 2 1

For Lisa Noecker,
a friend in deed

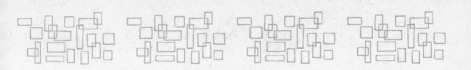

contents

foreword

I know what you're thinking.

Do we really need another etiquette book? Haven't we already been told to hold our pinkies high and refrain from nose-blowing at the table? Is there really more to be said about using the right fork, saying please and thank you, and avoiding heated political arguments at dinner parties?

Oh, if only it were that simple. But this, my hons, is an etiquette book for the *real world.* In these pages we deal with how to resist a playground smack-down with the Mom You Hate; how to behave when arrested; how to deal with low talkers, slow walkers, and a ceaseless stream of rude behavior that affects those of us who don't deal daily with finger bowls but are more likely confronted with the finger.

This is not your mama's etiquette guide. Those are marvelous and much needed but are far less likely to coach the clueless on real-world dilemmas like whether or not you should have sex when staying at a relative's house, how to deal with the freaks who won't vaccinate their kids, and "courtesy flushes"—they're not just for men anymore.

This is the book I have always wanted to write because, as I frequently tell Duh Hubby, "If everyone would just do what I told them to do, the world would be a much better place." High-handed and imperious? Mayhap. But if you really believe you have all the answers, which I do, why not share with the class?

In a world in which the admittedly fabulous Adele smacks gum at the Grammy Awards and M.I.A. insists upon shooting the bird to an unsuspecting Super Bowl audience, there's no such thing as too many etiquette books.

What does this etiquette book have that others don't?

In a word, *you*. You the exhausted, overworked, undervalued mommy. These are your issues; this is your life. It's not rude to drop a time-suck of a friend who only wants to dump her problems on you. It's not rude to respond to the braggarts and the blowhards with a well-timed and expertly delivered put-down. I have examples aplenty of how to navigate the tough stuff in this life with humor, wisdom, and—yes—profanity. While it may seem a bit antithetical to use quite so many "naughty words" in an etiquette book, I can assure you that I would never use curse words for shock value alone or to prop up a needy joke. We live in a world in which one Real Housewife of New Jersey seriously admonishes another to "show some fuckin' class!" Enough said.

There are lots of people to thank for making this book possible. Jennifer Enderlin, my editor at St. Martin's Press, got the ball rolling with not only the concept, but also some mighty fine suggestions along the way. You can thank her for the section on playdates. Thanks also to Jenny Bent, my ferociously talented agent of twelve years now, who never fails to take my calls, talk me out of the tree, and stroke me when I'm feeling frazzled. I heart those two broads.

Thanks also to friends and family for sending so many questions and ideas my way. The questions about etiquette included in each chapter came from informal interviews with friends, colleagues, and even some strangers. Based on those interviews, I quickly realized that some bad behavior is practically universal. Failure to RSVP (now the host has to call *you*—really?), insufferably braggy parents (including a phenomenon a friend calls "faux complaining;" for example, "Olivia bosses me around all day in French! Oh, those four-year-olds!"), and rude drivers were at the top of the list.

Whether it was over dinner with friends or a conversation with someone in line for a dressing room at T. J. Maxx, as soon as I said, "Hey, I'm writing an etiquette book. Which bad behavior bugs you most?" it was honestly hard to get them to shut up. Thank God!

Yes, him, too. Because at the end of the day, I do thank him for letting me live this lovely life in which I get to do exactly what I was put on this earth to do. I'll admit it's hard to picture a God in the sky looking down and pointing a bony finger and saying: "You! The pear-shaped Southern chick with the attitude—you can write funny stuff all day and be paid for it." I dodged a bullet. He could've chosen me to invent pajama jeans. So, well, whew.

And, finally, I want to thank everyone who reads my column, buys my books, and, most especially, takes the time to write me and let me know that it gave them a chuckle on a dreary day. Absolutely nothing makes me happier than hearing that. Okay, maybe the breadsticks at Olive Garden, but I swear, nothing else.

rude bitches make me tired

*

chapter 1

Check-Splitting:
Who Had the Gorgonzola Crumbles,
and Should We Really Care?

My friend Gray and I have often chuckled at the memory of how our mothers and grandmothers would agonize over splitting the check following the conclusion of a ladies' lunch on the town. Finally, at some point, one of the ladies would say to one member of the group, "Since you drove, we'll pay the tip."

Gray and I have been friends for three decades, ever since we met on the job at a daily newspaper where she was a photographer and I wrote feature stories about mules being born and the like. It's amazing that we were able to get jobs even though we were clearly very young children thirty years ago. Practically embryos. Anywho, it goes without saying that we have eaten many, many meals together in all kinds of restaurants and with all kinds of people over the years.

Because this is such a treasured bond between us, as soon as the check comes, one of us will chuckle and say to the other: "Since you drove . . ."

Maybe you have to be there.

The point is, we know that dividing the check at the restaurant can bring out all sorts of unintentionally rude behavior. At the heart of this sort of accidental etiquette breach is that it is ever so tacky to ever discuss money in public. It just is.

And while offering to pay the tip because gas was purchased by one of the members of the party is, on the face of it, a nice gesture, it only serves to muddy the waters.

How far must we carry this? As I write this, gas is about $3.44 a gallon in my hometown. If I take two friends to lunch downtown on our lovely riverfront, I've used no more than $1.10 in gas to pick them up.

This is less than the cost of a glass of sweet tea these days, so really, must we make it an issue? Should I point out that, because I drove, the rest of the lunch party owes me about one-fourth of the Caribbean Fudge Pie that I am, too, ordering even though my ass is spilling over either side of my chair.

No.

But still, in some quarters, you will hear all sorts of reasons why someone should pay a smaller percentage (or a higher one!) of the check when it arrives.

This is something that makes the server crazy. Hasn't she

already been sufficiently inconvenienced by your insistence that the check be split six ways and that approximately one and a half of you are going in together to pay for the seventh woman's bill because it's her birthday?

Where are my smelling salts?

Question: We go out to dinner about once a month on a Saturday night with two couples who live in our cul-de-sac. We really like everything about these couples except for the fact that they drink very expensive wines with dinner and my husband and I are teetotalers. When the bill arrives, you guessed it, they always split it three ways even though we just ordered chicken cutlets and water!

Okay, *you* guessed it: I don't need my smelling salts anymore; I need a very dry Grey Goose martini as big as my head. Ahh. There. Much better. Now, where were we? Oh, yes. You and your lushy fun friends sticking you with the wine bill . . .

First of all, let the record show that your couple-friends are assholes. Just because you share a driveway with someone doesn't mean that they should be your dinner companions. And, not to put too fine a point on this, but you and your husband sound like you'd be happier with your own kind. I mean, who the hell goes out to eat and orders a chicken cutlet and water on a Sadday night? I mean besides Garrison Keillor. For

Christ's sake, it's *Saturday night.* Live a little—get the osso bucco. Look it up.

I'm sorry. I don't for an instant mean to imply that just because you don't drink, you're no fun. I just want to come right out and say it: You're No Fun.

Assuming that you really do want to continue this pitiful dinner charade for your own weird reasons (swapping, perhaps?) I will answer your question.

You're going to have to speak up. Yes! Crazy and radical, I know! You're going to actually form the sentence in your empty noggin, feel the words in your mouth, and then hear them hang on the air.

Here's what you say:

"Roscoe and I didn't have wine, so y'all can split that and leave us out of it."

Man, oh, man, how I'd love to be a fly on the wall when that happens. Sorry. I was assuming this was a Denny's, but then I remembered the "fine wine" thing.

Their jaws will drop and they'll be shocked that, after many months of sticking you with a third of the fancy wine you didn't drink, the metaphorical scales have fallen from your eyes. Crappidy-doo-dah. Game over.

You see, they've been wondering what is wrong with you for all this time anyway. Are you so desperate for friends that you have to buy them? Because that's what you're doing every time you meekly fork over your credit card for your third of the bill. We're done here.

Almost . . .

Is there anything more agonizing than hearing a humiliating recitation of everything you've eaten by the number-crunching weirdo in your party?

"Madge, you had the arugula-beet salad, but you added on the gorgonzola crumbles for a dollar seventy-five, so . . . your share comes to . . ."

It is just such a terrible end to what could have been a lovely lunch or dinner. To hear your every lamb lollipop recounted (two at $11.95 each . . .) is simply horrifying.

The rule is simple: separate checks if appropriate (that means a party of six or fewer) and, for larger groups, a commitment to accepting that the bill should be split evenly.

There's often an outlier, of course. There's the pale friend who must have everything "gluten-free" or she will double over and collapse in a tower of her own shit mid-meal. This is always such a downer for the rest of the table. Maybe you could ask her to sit elsewhere? Like Indiana?

While we're still in the restaurant, so to speak, let's take a moment to remind one another that the waiter is there to do a job, not to hear about your "gastric bypass," "lactose intolerance," "gastroesophageal reflux," "homoerotica fantasies," and the like.

He or she also doesn't need to hear that if he accidentally gives you caffeinated coffee, your heart will fly out of your chest and sit on the table, thumping away, while all you and your lunch companions can do is watch until it finally, mercifully, stops.

Here's a tip: They don't care about your coffee preference. They asked you only because you expected it. The truth is, you'll get decaf if it's convenient, and if it's not, well, that's a mighty fine-looking aorta you got there.

Remember that it's important to tip generously, especially if you ever plan to return. Servers remember the cheap creep that ran 'em ragged and left a cool ten-spot for a hundred-dollar meal. You know who you are. For the love of Bobby Flay, tip for good service, tip for lousy service, just tip. Some of y'all can be pretty demanding.

Example: "We need more bread. And when you get back, I'm going to think up a few other things we need, but I'm only going to list them one at a time so you have to make a bunch of trips."

Just remember: These servers can do awful things to your food right before it comes out. Awful things.

That's Not a Salad Fork, You Stupid Bitch

A lot of people get confused when they're in a nice restaurant and there are, like, a million forks surrounding their plates.

There's no reason to fret. Generally speaking, silver is placed in the order of its use, so you pick up the piece on the outside first. See? That wasn't so hard, was it?

When you've finished eating (or, as we say in the South, "had a sufficiency"), avoid announcing this by saying, loudly, "Damn, I'm stuffed!" or worse, "I'm chewin' high." There's no need to announce the state of your stomach. No one is interested, and the notion that you need to give alerts—as though, if you lifted your shirt, a fuel gauge just like your car has would be revealed with a wand wavering between E and F—is truly off-putting. Along these lines, never, ever burp and then say "Yay! Room for more!"

That said, when you're finished, really finished, not just talking about how full you are and continuing to shovel it in, place your fork on your plate, prongs down, beside your knife with the blade facing the fork. I am, too, serious. Good table etiquette is all that separates us from Kardashians— er, savages.

Some other tips . . . Always break bread with your fingers; never cut it with a knife. The bread knife is just for buttering and is also dreadfully unhandy for stabbing intruders; trust me.

A word about artichokes: Don't ever order them. Nobody looks good sucking on leaves. Not even a koala bear, and damn sure not you.

Know your limits: Don't order lobster, tails-on shrimp,

Cornish game hen, and so forth, in a nice restaurant. You're going to look like a doofus no matter how hard you try not to, and it honestly doesn't help when you insist "I eat this shit all the time. Really." Ditto ordering something you don't know how to pronounce.

Good: "French onion soup."

Bad: "Duck cawn-fit."

A word about finger bowls: Okay, don't freak out when you see one for the first time, Gomer. And don't take a bath in it, either. Just dab the tips of your fingers in the bowl, and for the love of God, don't try to make a joke by also dabbing at your underarms and crotch.

Okay, maybe the underarms. That's actually pretty funny sometimes.

Don't talk with your mouth full. Don't talk with your mouth full. Don't talk with your mouth full.

Now. Since you drove . . .

chapter 2

✳

Funerals: Now Is Not the Time for Store-Bought Cakes and Backless Maxi Dresses from Forever 21

Okay, let's just get the most important stuff out of the way first. Never, ever take a store-bought cake to the bereaved family. I don't want to hear that you know an "amazing bakery, really the best!" or that "everybody does it, so what's the big deal?"

Y'all are going straight to hell for thinking like that. This is a funeral, not some godless Unitarian Universalist potluck.

Look, I get that you're terribly busy, which also explains why you never visited poor, dowdy, and now quite dead Aunt Fern while she was alive. Yes, you were so, so busy. There simply wasn't time.

Sure, she could be a handful. Everyone knows that. She was dotty as hell and, toward the last, spent twelve hours a day watching *Law & Order* reruns. When you did visit, she spent the first thirty minutes accusing you of things and the second thirty minutes proving why she was right. But she's dead now, and you better rustle something up quick.

And please quit whining about how Fern was so inconsiderate as to die on the weekend when your teenage son's traveling soccer team was in the play-offs and just who did she think she was anyway?

I'll tell you who: Fern was the one who showed up at your mama's baby shower with a stack of crocheted blankets that she made just for you. Your mama still has them because they were the dearest thing on earth to her. Fern's arthritic hands crocheted those blankies for you all those years ago, and you can't even toss together a little flour, sugar, and baking powder in her honor?

The phrase "trifling heifer" springs to mind.

Let me be clear. I'm not saying that you have to bake a cake for the family. I'm saying that you do have to do something that honors Fern's memory properly. This will never include a ghastly spice cake from Food King with a big orange carrot clumsily piped on the top and a list of unpronounceable ingredients as long as the book of Revelation. And it's not much better to do that cake-mix thing where you try to make it look like you actually creamed butter and sugar and gave much of a shit.

Whatever you take to the family should be made by your own two hands. Don't make me mention those hand-crocheted blankets again. Simply stated: Any idiot can bake a ham, and a ham is always a welcome addition since it can be both centerpiece for the luncheon after the service and used in biscuits for the morning after. Here's how you do it:

Ham Fit for a Funeral

1 (6- to 8-pound) fully cooked bone-in ham

48 whole cloves

1-pound box light brown sugar

1 cup spicy brown mustard

1 cup cola (I'm a Coke girl, but Pepsi will do fine.)

¾ cup bourbon (Well, it is a Southern recipe,
   now, isn't it?)

Preheat the oven to 350 degrees Fahrenheit. Remove the skin from the ham and trim the fat to ¼-inch thickness. This will keep the ham moist while it cooks. Make shallow cuts in the fat ¾ inch apart in a diamond pattern. Stick the cloves in the centers of each diamond.

Put the ham in a lightly greased 13-by-9-inch pan. Stir together the brown sugar, mustard, cola, and bourbon. Spoon this mixture over the ham.

Bake at 350 degrees on the lowest oven rack for 2 hours and 30 minutes, basting with pan juices every 15 to 20 minutes. Remove the ham from the oven and let stand 20 minutes before slicing. You can baste the ham a bit as it rests to give it a glossy look.

This is my go-to ham recipe, and it came from *Southern Living* magazine, which, along with the fabulous *Garden & Gun,* should be on your coffee table at all times, praise Jesus.

It should be noted that I'm assuming that Aunt Fern was a Christian woman, which is why I suggested ham. If she was of the Jewish persuasion, as my grandmother would say, may I suggest a lovely platter of latkes or a nice brisket? I don't have any Jewish recipes because I'm a Methodist, but some of my best friends are Jewish, and I can ask if you need me to. Really, it's no bother.

While we're talking about funeral food, if there's one thing that pisses off a bereaved family, it's being saddled with the hellish chore of returning dishes to people who brought food in nondisposable containers.

These inconsiderate assholes usually trot in, place the food down, and say, "Oh, you can just get that platter back to me whenever it's convenient."

How magnanimous of you. Look, not all families are blessed enough to have a gay son who lives for this kind of thing, making notations of china patterns in a notebook and cross-referencing with the name of the dish and the hands that prepared it.

No, most of us muddle through in a grief-soaked haze, and three weeks after everybody's gone and the surviving spouse is resigned to watching *Wheel* by herself and getting entirely too many calls from her idiot sister-in-law, she realizes that her kitchen counter is full of dishes of unknown origin. The burden is so great that she might, just for one horrible second, contemplate blowing her brains out right there on the kitchen Congoleum so she won't have to deal with them.

Yes, I know your deviled eggs look so much prettier in your heirloom egg platter with the little porcelain chicks on the handles, but do you think the bereaved should worry about babying your precious porcelain and making sure you get it back in a timely fashion?

Actually, in any situation—not just ones involving the stopping of a human heart—it's advisable to take food in containers that are obviously not meant to be returned. It's why God made GladWare. And we're mighty glad he did. Oh, and don't you dare put one of those little address labels St. Jude sent you on GladWare. Nobody's going to return a plastic container. That sort of behavior lets me know you probably took those labels and never even sent any money to St. Jude.

Question: Is it ever okay to email condolences? I just learned that my cousin died, and while we weren't very close, I'd like to do something.

Oh, why not just text your condolences? You could say something like

Sorry 4 ur loss.):

I mean, why be so formal as a telephone call or a card or letter or flowers? It's just a death, after all. It's not like you forgot to DVR the season finale of *The Voice*.

No. It is not okay to email condolences. Ever.

Question: I am going to a visitation at the funeral home for a guy I used to work with and I'm a little anxious about it. Can you help?

I imagine you're anxious because you're afraid there might be an open casket and looking at dead people wearing too much foundation is creepier than tonguing your cousin. Yeah, I said it. Point is, I totally understand how off-putting it is to be in a room with the freshly dead. But in some families, this is tradition, and you have to respect that. I find it useful to picture everyone in the room naked. No, sorry. That's what I do when making speeches. What I meant to say was that it's useful to engage in conversation with the non-dead people in the room. Don't linger. There isn't a Chinese buffet in the corner. Just get in, tell the family you're sorry, shake some hands, share a warm memory of the deceased, and get out. This should take no longer than fifteen minutes. Set your watch if you must.

Question: I can't attend the funeral of a church friend, but my husband plans to go. Is it okay for him to

write both our names in the guest book? If he does, it's possible that the family will think I attended. I don't mean to be disingenuous, but what's the real harm?

I'm sure you're expecting me to pronounce this tacky, but that would be extremely hypocritical, since I've done the same thing myself. Look, I baked the damn ham. I don't owe this person my entire life. Still, tongues will wag if they know I skipped the funeral to go to the outlets with my best friend from high school who is in town for only one day. Okay, three, but still . . .

I guess what I'm trying to say is that—and it *kills* me to say this—I can't pass judgment on you, because I've done the same thing. In a case like this, let your conscience be your guide. I asked my conscience, and it agreed that the dearly departed would not want me to miss the 65 percent off sale today only at the Kate Spade outlet. If your conscience is a bit more, uh, active than mine, then, well, you should be turning in your hymnal to page 353 right about now.

Question: Should I attend the funeral of my ex-husband's father? I always loved the man and I think he loved me, too. I don't want to make waves, but I'd like to pay my respects.

Unless there is a compelling reason not to go (his widow hates your guts and loves to tell everybody you broke her son's heart, for instance), I don't see why not. Don't try to sit with the family, though. Even if you had kids with your ex, take a discreet seat in the back, listen attentively, cry gently, and remember the good times you shared with this dear man.

Question: So, bottom line—black only at a funeral, or can we finally relax the rules a bit?

I know why you're asking. You're just itchin' to wear that age-inappropriate yellow chiffon maxi dress you bought at Forever 21 the other day at the mall, aren't you? You really shouldn't. Not because it's yellow but because it's backless. Ick.

Actually, you don't have to wear black to funerals if you don't want to. Most mainstream religions are fine with dark colors. The trick is to look respectfully somber. Avoid floral prints and similar silliness. As always, it's much easier for men: Wear a suit.

In some cases, the obituary provides guidance. A trend of late is to invite attendees to "dress comfortably." Again, do not take this as a license to wear booty shorts and your favorite Kenny F*&!#ing Powers T-shirt.

Question: What's with obituaries lately? The other day I, swear to God, saw one in which two adult children were scolded from the grave as "perpetually ungrate-

ful and inattentive." It wasn't the first time I've seen
something like that. Is this a trend?

Could be. Just this week, I saw an obituary for a Charlotte,
North Carolina, woman that read much like the one you just
described. One child was singled out as "the good one" (also,
I'm quite sure, the one who placed the obituary in the newspaper), and another was termed "a tremendous source of
heartbreak over the years." I can't state strongly enough that
this—while compelling reading that makes you call your best
friend as soon as you're sure she's awake and ask, "Did you
read this shit?"—is an abomination.

There's no way to be sure if this was the wish of the deceased or if it was planted by the Chosen One to tweak his
siblings. I hope it was the latter because, frankly, I can't picture Saint Peter swinging the gates wide for such a mean-
spirited old cow, you feel me?

chapter 3

Sky Mauled:

How to Survive Airline Travel Without

Compromising Your Good Manners

There is perhaps no place on this big blue marble where manners are tromped upon with more frequency and variety than the world of airline travel. Tromp. Tromp. Tromp.

And while I appreciate the importance of homeland security, I do *not* appreciate having my middle-age body scanned in public with less privacy than is afforded at the gynecologist's office.

The first affront is the public removal of shoes. Ghastly. But do it we must, and I try to put on my "big-girl panties" and quietly submit. (By the by, I've flown quite a bit this year, and *all* my panties are big-girl panties because every time I'm in an airport, the Cinnabon staff chases me down, flings me to the ground, and force-feeds a series of buns and crumb cakes into my gullet. Really, they're quite aggressive. Somebody should do something.)

I've finally caught on that slip-on shoes or sandals are far preferable so you don't end up spending ten minutes on a cold metal folding chair lacing and buckling and so forth. I hate flats and I hate wearing flip-flops anywhere but the beach, but (deep breaths) it's really the best way.

It's times like this when I remember my very first flight. It was a family vacation to California in the early '70s. This was when people still dressed up for airplane travel (think shantung suits for the ladies, pocket squares for the gentlemen) and there was a better-than-average chance that you'd be served a decent hollandaise at some point on the flight. Compare and contrast with the way most people dress for a flight these days: a sweatshirt that simply says COLLEGE for the men and, for ladies, anything that has the word PINK scrawled on the backside.

Who can blame these fliers? Why dress up when you know you're going to be wanded, frisked, and essentially felt up in public just to board the plane? My last TSA screening was so intrusive via wand, X-ray, and full-body scan that I called to cancel this year's mammogram.

During this "violation" segment of preboarding, the old advice to "think of England" comes to mind. But even that doesn't work, because that would require a transatlantic flight. . . .

So there you are, barefoot, walking on some disgusting rubber mat behind the sketchy dude with the fungal toes, your body scanned to a fare-thee-well, and now there is still the final indignity: actually boarding the airplane and flying.

Once on board, it's important to follow a few basic etiquette rules to make things better for your fellow fliers.

- Move briskly to your seat. Do not stand there, clutching your ticket in your sweaty little hand, looking up at the numbers and letters identifying the row and seats as though you honestly don't know what they mean. You're a forensic accountant, for God's sake. Don't act like you inhaled stupid dust and suddenly can't decipher these mysterious hieroglyphics overhead. Your seat is 15A. Find it and sit the fuck down so the rest of us can do the same.

- Once you have located your seat, do not spend more than a scant few seconds placing your paraphernalia in the overhead compartment. Do not place your puffy ski jacket or similar clothing into this compartment, because this just confirms what a dick you are. The overhead space is limited (duh) and clothing can easily be smushed under the seat in front of you. Also, always use the compartment near your seat. Do *not* stow your carry-on in the fourth row when you're seated in the twenty-sixth row.

This will lead to embarrassing intercom announcements from the flight attendant asking for the "douche sitting in the back row who placed his crap in the front of the plane" to please retrieve it. Happens all the time.

- Once you sit down, do not try to talk to me. I don't want to chat. I just want to sit here, reading my magazine and feeling the magic of a well-timed Xanax purr through my frazzled brain. I don't fly to socialize with strangers. Besides, you forget that I've seen your toes.

- I know this may sound silly, but you should try to feign attention when the flight attendant is going through his or her spiel. Of course you know how to fasten a seat belt. But when we're all bobbing in the waves and you're wondering how I knew about the whole seat cushion as flotation device thing, I ain't sharing. You will not be like Leo DiCaprio clinging to the side of my plywood. I will flick you off like a wolf spider. Buh-bye.

- If you have to get up at any time during the flight, use the armrests to hoist your fat ass up and about. Do *not* grab the headrest of the seat in front of you. That is my hair you're pulling out by the roots. Don't make me ask the pilot to pull this plane over.

Damn! It's Crowded up in Here

Now more than ever, airlines are hell-bent to fill every single seat. Gone is the day when you could view your decidedly sucky middle-seat, rear-of-plane assignment as temporary because, once airborne, you could cheerfully upgrade to a better seat, one with a window and without such noxious proximity to the shitter.

You know how you always spend forever waiting at the gate even though it seems that everyone has boarded? The delay is often explained by the dulcet tones of the pilot, who may mention that "we" are waiting for runway clearance *or* for a gate to open up at the destination *or* the ever-popular "weather, yeah, just weather," but I believe it's because someone has sent the flight attendants into the terminal to snatch random bodies to fill any empty seats.

I swear on a recent flight to Charlotte they drafted two Quiznos workers and the weird lady in the restroom who expects a dollar for handing you a Kleenex to make sure there wasn't a single open seat. Done. Flight attendants, please take your seats.

This full-flight-or-bust attitude has created all sorts of discomfort for those of us doomed to sit behind the Recline Monster.

Entitled Recline Monster has paid for his seat and he gets

to recline if he wants to. I mean, there's a recline button right there. If reclining were so rude, wouldn't they remove that button the same way they sealed up those tiny ashtrays that used to be in the armrest?

Technically, yes. Recline Monster has every right to recline. It's just incredibly ill-mannered. It's the same with taking smelly food aboard. The TSA can't stop you from taking that garlic-and-onion calzone on board even though it smells like an incendiary device. But just because you can do something legally, it doesn't mean you should.

Recline Monster abruptly reclines all the way for his maximum comfort, sending your laptop into your muffin top and your Sprite every damn where. He careth not a whit. It is all about his needs, which at least momentarily are fulfilled. It is nappy time for Recline Monster. What to do?

First, please don't do what the pissed-off passenger on a flight from Washington, D.C., to Ghana did recently. Perhaps he had spent months silently seething at various Recline Monsters and he finally snapped. The passenger just hit Recline Monster on the top of his empty head as hard as he could.

Unfortunately, the TSA gets super cranky when one passenger assaults another, so the whole flight had to be canceled and I'm guessing the guy who did the hitting was given major stink eye from the disgruntled passengers having to deplane.

I don't advise slapping Recline Monster, because violence is never the answer. I do, however, advise a slow, deliberate, and steady kicking of his seatback for the duration of the flight. It'll drive him nuts, and if he complains, just explain that Dr. Oz said on TV that if you don't move your legs on a flight, you could develop a deadly blood clot. You can up the ante by mentioning that Dr. Oz was speaking person-ally, just to you, through the TV, when he said that and you can make your eyes look all googly like a certified crazy person.

I'm guessing, because I am not a "1 percenter," to use the political parlance, that reclining seats aren't an issue in first class, where the air smells rather like fat leather wallets and warmed butter cookies. Bitter, party of me. And speaking of the rich folk . . .

Question: Why did everybody get so pissy at me when I wouldn't shut off my cell phone? I was in the middle of a very important game of Words with Friends, and what's more, I am a Very Important Actor. Just ask my brothers, if you can remember any of their names. Hahahahaha!—Alec Baldwin

Oh, Alec. May I call you Mr. Baldwin? I used to be such a huge fan of your work. The scenes in *30 Rock* with your ghastly TV mama, Elaine Stritch, kept me in, well, "stritches"!

But this stunt you pulled on that L.A.-to-N.Y. flight where you were rude to a flight attendant simply trying to do her job and then tweeted about it like you were the victim?

Don't you think we'd *all* like to be playing *Words with Friends* on our magic phone boxes while awaiting takeoff? Do you think you're somehow exempt from the rules of the airways? And, more to the point, what the hell are you doing flying commercial instead of by private jet? Don't you know a Travolta or someone who could fly your curiously wide ass across the country whenever you need it? Hmmmm?

Question: I'm never quite sure which armrest is mine. I don't want to appear rude and take the wrong armrest. Of course, I'd really like to just take both, but something tells me that's not good etiquette. Can you help?

"Whose armrest is it, anyway?" is a great question. The answer is that they are all mine. All right, not really. The truth is, they are all Alec Baldwin's. No, really. Here's the rule: If you are on the aisle, you get the aisle armrest; if you are on the window, you get the right; if you are in the middle, you get both. It's only fair because the middle is a craptastic location and everybody knows it. So, middle seater, sit down, stake your claim on both armrests, and never let go. Not even to eat your fifteen-dollar "salad."

**_Question: I once heard someone say that noisy children
should be safely stowed in the overhead compartment.
Is that true?_**

Yes. Yes, it is. This is a little-known rule that is really
pressed into service only after the child in question, usually a
scrawny long-haired little turd named Mendelssohn or some
such, has been repeatedly kicking your seat and using his
outdoor voice while his clueless parents do nothing but af-
firm his "specialness." He is not special. He is just another
privileged little snot whose parents were way too old when
they had him and now he runs the show. Press the Call button and ask the flight attendant to stow his obnoxious ass
overhead. Owing to the ski jackets you insisted on storing
overhead, you won't even hear his muffled screams. Winning!

chapter 4

The Grand Old (Dinner) Party: Bring Wine and Trivia

'm a huge fan of the dinner party, as long as I don't have to host it, of course. As a matter of fact, Duh Hubby and I have become quite adept at soaking up invites without reciprocating. It's the height of rudeness, but it does make life so much less complicated, yes?

So our New Year's resolution this year was to do better, and by that, I mean to realize that while we consider ourselves to be exemplary dinner party guests (translation: we totally bring on the banter, and more important, we know when to leave), we realize that we've been selfish creatures and must return every invitation with a soiree of our own, or at least a few of them.

Right now, there are several friends who are laughing at this and saying, "Ha! It'll never happen."

It's true. We tend to round up everyone we "know and

owe" and throw a big backyard get-together every so often that, we feel, takes care of the social obligation without the endless menu-planning, napkin-ironing, silver-polishing woes of actually hosting a proper dinner party.

Do as I say, not as I do, or did. Really, we promise to do better, starting . . . now.

Question: Every time we host a dinner party, my friend asks who else is going to be there before she says whether or not she'll come. This makes me absolutely furious. I usually say: "We're still asking folks, so I'm not really sure." If she persists, I make an excuse and hang up. She's implying that we're not interesting enough company by ourselves, isn't she?

Oh, my, yes. Let's just stipulate that your friend was raised by wolves. And not the kind of wolves who use fine china and cloth napkins, the real rowdy kind that devours Boy Scouts on a forest camporee. Someone really should've told her this is extremely rude. That said, there might be a reason for her crassness. I'm thinking maybe she's a single lady and she's terrified that you're doing another one of your ambush-style fix-ups with one of your dreadfully dull cousins, what with their male pattern baldness and Klan Nazi tattoos. Am I getting warm?

I'm giving her the benefit of the doubt here. If she's a married lady, then we're back to our wolves theory. Look, I don't like the way she's acting, but there's a very simple solution. Before you invite her, have a good working understanding of who has accepted and start the invitation with "We're having a dinner party on the twenty-sixth! We'd love for you to come. Bill and Marge are coming, and so are Julian and Kate. Can you make it?"

If she says, "Anybody else coming?" you are within your rights to simply hang up on her impossibly rude ass.

Question: My husband and I argue about this all the time. If we take an expensive (really!) wine to a dinner party, is it rude of the host to put it aside for themselves instead of serve it to the guests? I say it is; he says it isn't.

If you take an expensive wine and hand it over to your host, he has the right to (really!) *(a)* smash it against the wall if he likes, *(b)* gush and open it immediately, or *(c)* say, "Wow! I love this stuff, but we can never afford it!" and hide it in the washing machine so others can't find it.

Simply stated: A gift is a gift. If your host wants to peel off the label and wipe his naughties with it, it's his decision, disgusting as that might be.

And while we're on the subject of party libations, to those guests who drink other people's pricey microbrews when all they brought to the party was a two-pack of Busch: This isn't college anymore. Grow up already.

Question: How do you deal with couples who stay too long at a dinner party? We have two sets of friends that we almost hate to invite because they routinely stay at least two hours after everyone else has left.

Two hours?!? They must find themselves quite charming indeed. As sure as some blunderbuss is going to break at least one piece of your aunt Tink's wedding china, there will always be stragglers at a dinner party. You could take this as an enormous compliment (they're having such a good time, they don't want the night to end!), but I realize that you just want them to get the hell out so you can finally watch your DVR'd *Young & the Restless* and unwind after a day of exhausting party preparation. I'm always amazed that people think that a dinner invitation is anything more than that. If you've given them two extra hours of witty companionship, that's about ninety minutes too much.

Simply stand up, yawn dramatically, and say: "We're so glad you could come, but we are tired and we're going to bed now. Good night."

I've actually used this line on more than one occasion, and it's extremely effective. Remember: Some people really think that you can't get enough of them. They need a not-so-gentle reminder that, essentially, nothing could be further from the truth.

Question: I don't like icebreaker questions at dinner parties. They always feel like a performance. Can't I just have my shrimp cocktail in a martini glass without all the yammering?

Well, no. If the hostess wants to get folks talking, especially when most party guests are meeting one another for the first time, an icebreaker can be a wonderful thing.

I once went to a lovely dinner party where the hostess asked us, one by one, "If you were hosting a dinner party and you could invite three people, living or dead, whom would you invite?"

I immediately responded "living" because I'm all about the cheap, easy laugh. But as the topic bounded from guest to guest, I have to admit it was fascinating. To a point.

The woman across the table from me went first: "I'd invite Jesus Christ, Adolf Hitler, and Gandhi."

I wanted to call bullshit on that because you could tell she really wanted to invite the Real Housewives of Beverly Hills, but she was afraid that would make her sound as dumb as, well, one of the Real Housewives of Beverly Hills.

The table cooed appreciatively at such a clever trio of imaginary guests. I knew my turn was coming up, and all I could think of, seriously, was Miley Cyrus.

The next guest delicately patted the corners of his mouth with a napkin, although there was nothing there to begin with, and cleared his throat: "I'd like to invite my maternal and paternal grandmothers, both of whom died ten years ago, and I'd like to invite my fiancée so she could see how wonderful they were."

Everyone did a big "awwww," and the fiancée's eyes glistened with adoration. She did that thing where you put your fingers on your eyes to keep from crying. Ever notice how people do that and then stare at their fingers? What are they expecting to see? Ketchup? Nope, it's tears.

The long-dead-grandmother bit is a can't-miss at a dinner party icebreaker. Now, when it was my turn, I needed to remember that Jesus *and* the dead grandmother had been taken. Shit.

A woman with a gorgeous upsweep was next. "Well, Jesus, of course," she said.

"Nuh-*uh*! Somebody already used Jesus!" I said way too loud; plus I think some mashed potatoes sprayed out of my mouth in a most unattractive fashion.

The hostess handled my faux pas with such grace. "Oh, you can use Jesus as often as you like," she said, giving me a look that said maybe I should be thinking harder.

The table continued merrily along with a few more Jesuses, some more dead relatives, and not a sign of Miley Cyrus or, my second thought, Dina Lohan.

It was my turn. It was my come-to-you-know-who moment. Would I be true to myself, or would I fake it and try to impress everyone by claiming genuine interest in chatting up

Mahatma Gandhi, Fyodor Dostoevsky, and Thomas Jefferson? Talk about your garden-variety snorefest.

"Well," I finally said. "That guy's grandmothers sounded pretty cool . . . oh, and Dina Lohan."

Please learn from my horrible mistake. Bone up on current events and always have a top-three answer ready.

Question: How can I politely extricate myself from a dinner party guest who wants to monopolize my time for the entire evening? I don't mind a five-minute chat, but I want to talk to other people. What do I do about this human Velcro?

That's easy. After a few minutes of banter, gently guide Velcro over to another party guest, introduce them with a quick "Biff, here, also likes to discuss the relative merits of different brands of raised white-letter radial tires. . . ." Biff will hate your ass for a very long time, but that's not your problem. No hurt feelings *and* you can finally grab some of that fabulous bruschetta! If you can't get away (he's seated beside you at a formal dinner, for example), make the best of it by talking to the person across from you or to the other side as well as to Velcro Man. Short of grabbing the gravy boat and pouring its contents into your lap, you're trapped.

Question: What on earth is gluten, and why do all of my dinner party guests whine about how they're allergic to it? How could they suddenly be allergic to something they've eaten all their lives?

Gluten, to answer your question, is a substance present in cereal grains, especially wheat, which is responsible for the elastic texture of dough. One symptom of gluten intolerance is an annoying whining sound heard when talking to a dinner party guest. Gluten, it turns out, is in damn near every processed food. Who knew?

People have gone a little anti-gluten nutso, if you ask me. You can't throw a rock without hitting someone who whines about their newly discovered allergy to gluten. Go ahead; try it. You see them in the grocery store, dutifully poring over the ingredients list or taking the frozen-foods manager to task for not stocking more gluten-free tostadas. As far as I can tell, the biggest side effect of a gluten sensitivity is that you actually become the number one symptom: a huge pain in the ass.

The truth is, 1 in 133 people actually has celiac disease (a genuinely serious and unpleasant intestinal ailment hugely aggravated by gluten), so if you host a dinner party, you should just invite 132 people. Problem solved.

Seriously, the issue of special diets can strangle a decent dinner party. You can't be expected to accommodate Blanche's vegan diet, Raoul's imaginary gluten allergy, David's kosher requirements, and so on. Just tell 'em what you're having, and if they're freaked out, tell 'em to bring something they can eat. Oh, and a really expensive bottle of wine for you to hide in the washing machine because they are stressing the shit out of you.

chapter 5

*

Gym Etiquette:
Or, "Pardon Me, But Is This
Your Ass Sweat?"

Is there anything more dispiriting than realizing that you just sat down in a pool of someone else's ass sweat?

The gymnasium, to use prissy parlance, is ground zero for myriad etiquette violations, most involving the unwanted sharing of bodily fluids and odors.

While I've maintained numerous gym memberships in the past, I must confess that I found them to all be extremely cost prohibitive, on account of I never actually went to the gym.

That's not true. I went twice and then realized that it was a lot more fun to use that hour to grab a chocolate croissant and chai tea instead. Mornings can be so stressful.

Loyal readers will recall that I did attempt a weekly yoga class but was put off by the incessant and unrepentant pooting of those around me. I still love the yoga clothes, though, and have become one of those poseurs who runs errands in full workout regalia even though I haven't technically worked out since the Clinton administration.

As a pear-shaped woman, I should be concentrating on squats for my glutes and the rest of it. A recent study found that pear-shaped women are more likely to have memory problems as we age than the so-called apple-shaped women who carry their fat in their tummies, not their hips.

If I had a personal trainer, I'd ask him or her just what sense that makes. Geographically speaking, the brain is a lot closer to the waist than it is to the butt. Soooo, ipso facto, presto change-o, if fat is clogging up your brain and causing memory loss, why wouldn't it be a bigger problem churning its way to the brain from the much-closer, uh, waistal area? Well, science community? I'm waiting, here.

Is it actually possible that, just as some ill-mannered readers have suggested to me over the years, all my brains are in my ass?

It doesn't seem fair that the location of my fat is going to make me forget stuff as I get older. Actually, I'm pretty sure that it's already started. I was going to tell you a story to illustrate this, but I forget.

So big butt equals bad memory. Maybe one day Jennifer Lopez and I can hang out with our big butts and forget stuff together. She might want to start with *Maid in Manhattan*— just saying.

Bottom line (ha!): I will be going back to the gym really, really someday, having now realized that those extra pounds aren't going to come off by themselves. Neither are they going to come off as long as I consider chicken-fried steak with a side of the theater-size box of Junior Mints to be a balanced dinner.

A trainer and gym regimen will get me back on track, and before you know it, I'll be as full of memories as my apple-shaped friends. It's on, bitches!

Question: I'm an older woman who attends a lunchtime aerobics class at the local Y. A very fit young woman in the class dresses very inappropriately, preferring those ghastly "butt floss" leotards to the traditional leggings and oversized T-shirts worn by the rest of us. Is there a delicate way to approach her?

Well, you could just pull her aside and say something on the order of, "I'm so sorry to say this, dear, but your ass cheeks are quite distracting and we really wish that you would just put them away." She will likely be offended by this, but you should just maintain a concerned maternal tone throughout. She will probably say something like, "You're just jealous!" and, of course, she's right. Comfort yourself with the knowledge that she won't always look like that. It's really all that any of us can cling to at times like this.

Question: I saw a man spit into the water fountain after his workout the other day. Should I report him?

Yes, and quickly. Spitting into the water fountain is one of the vilest etiquette offenses at the gym. (That, and refilling your oversized water bottle at the fountain when there's a line.) Spitting, along with excessive grunting by men lifting weights and wearing wide-legged shorts that broadcast their bidness, seems to result from some wrongheaded belief that they are real cavemen. For one hour a day, they and all the sweaty, grunting men don't have to think about how they have to pick up Lunchables and pantyliners at the store when they leave the gym. For this tiny window of time, they aren't worried about any of that. They are *men,* doing *manly* things. If it weren't so gross, it would almost be cute.

Question: A couple of women in my Pilates class talk on their cell phones during class, and it is beyond irritating to those of us who don't want to listen to their prattle. Shouldn't there be a "no cell phone" rule in class?

Absolutely. And not just in class but especially in the locker room, where pervs with phones can take pictures of folks milling about in their all-togethers, as I like to call the naked human body on the unfortunate occasions I am forced to think about its existence. Cell phones are discussed in another chapter, so

I will only say that to talk on one during a workout class is rude to classmates and to the instructor, who shouldn't have to stand there at the door, taking up phones like the drama teacher did in *High School Musical.* Grow up, assholes.

Question: Every time I lift weights, there's a guy who tells me I'm doing it all wrong. I know that I'm doing it right and that he's the wrong one. What should I do?

Stop working out with your husband. Next.

Question: I love the spinning room at our local fitness club, but what I don't love is listening to the TV overhead. Actually, this also bothers me in the lounge at the car dealership and even the hospital waiting room. Doesn't anybody read anymore?

Oh, if there's a God in heaven . . . but back to your point. I sympathize with this because just this week I was forced to endure a cartoon called *Happy Tree Friends* on the overhead TV at the tire store. The TV is set way up high to prevent people from changing channels or the volume. So there we sit, held prisoner like that scene in *A Clockwork Orange* where the guy has his eyes clipped open. And, yes, I could walk away just as you could pursue another gym activity, but why should I (you) have to?

Listen to your iPod while you spin away, and crank it up loud enough to drown out Fox News, *Murder, She Wrote,* or similar torture.

Question: I work out on my lunch hour, and when I'm at the club, I don't have time for conversation. I'm not there to be social; I'm there to work out. How can I communicate this without being rude?

From what I hear from my friends who work out, this is a huge problem. It basically comes down to whether you are retired or still working. The retirees consider the gym a fabulous place to work out a little, enjoy a smoothie, and catch up with folks they recognize while those folks are working out. It sounds wonderful unless you're trying to complete a cycle and you can't even get started for the incessant yammering from your "friend" as he chats while you're desperately trying to finish your elliptical workout.

Every so often, a situation presents itself in which it's simply not possible to spare feelings. You must be direct and say: "I'm sorry, but I don't have time to talk. I need to finish this workout on a schedule or I'll be late getting back to work."

Big-boy stuff, I know.

If you're not brave enough for this sort of direct answer (i.e., you are a Southerner), you can just try ignoring them until they get the hint. While they chat, you continue your workout, only very occasionally nodding yes or no to whatever inane question is being asked. This conveys that you really don't have time to talk, and sooner or later, they'll wander away to hassle somebody else. Just remember not to be too judgy, because one day, that'll be you approaching a "sorta friend" at the gym, clutching that fat stack of Kiwanis pancake supper tickets to sell. Circle of life, dude.

Question: I have a locker room dilemma! I understand that some people are more comfortable with their bodies than others, but why would anyone think I wanted to talk to them while they're just standing in front of me butt naked? Put a towel on!

I remember the first time I worked out at the Y. Being naturally repressed like any good Southern woman, I was horrified to see the old women wandering about with their gray matching carpet and drapes, so to speak, as though they didn't even know they were naked. While I carefully changed clothes in the shower like some kind of Baptist, they just laughed and conversed with absolute abandon. They weren't even wearing shower shoes!

Look, there will always be people with varying degrees of modesty. You can't ask them to put some clothes on, although you should mention under your breath in a high-handed tone that failure to wear shower shoes is just asking for athlete's foot, which is a *lifetime affliction*. They may brand you Debbie Downer for such comments, but that's not your concern.

As you get more comfortable speaking out, ask them to "For the love of God, sit on a towel in the sauna," or ask, "Are you seriously going to get in the pool with that oozing sore?" Some people require a little direction. Focus less on the offensive nudity and more on the hygiene of it all. Better?

Question: Why won't people put the dumbbells back where they found them? Is that really too much to ask? I'm tired of being everyone's nagging mother at the gym.

Oh, I suspect you're everyone's nagging mother wherever you go. But, yes, it is rude not to return equipment (dutifully wiped of sweat) to its original location. Equipment such as barbells, hand weights, and bands are dangerous lying around, waiting to trip someone, so this is a matter for the paid staff to handle. Tell them as often as necessary. Granted, they are probably talking to their boyfriend on the phone and too busy to deal with you, but keep at it. Mention potential lawsuits. Also how they really should eat more vegetables, go to bed earlier, and stop hanging around that rough crowd.

Question: What can I do about a "lurker"? Sometimes I'm resting between sets; it doesn't mean I'm ready to give up the machine. Can I just say, "Go away"?

Nobody likes a lurker, but on the other hand, this isn't your very own personal machine with a little brass plate on it with your name on it, so you might want to check yourself. If you're "resting" five minutes between sets, you're hogging the equipment. Mix up the workout and move to another machine or be prepared to hear "You done here?" a whole lot. Followed by, "How 'bout now? You done here?" and, if you continue to sit your resting ass on that machine, "How 'bout now? You done here, bitch?" Hey, I'm on their side.

chapter 6

Baby Steps:
Is She Pregnant or Is That a
Booze-Inflated Liver? Hint: Don't Ask!

Oh, baby.

You thought you were just happy about being a mommy, and now here I come, ready to tell you that pregnancy, childbirth, and the first few years of life are just one big-ass etiquette minefield.

Read on . . .

Question: Ever since I started showing, total strangers have come up to me in the supermarket or post office and asked if they could touch my belly! I can't imagine such rude behavior, can you?

Well, yes, I can. Listen, when I got pregnant at age forty, I was so thrilled that I actually asked strangers if they would like to touch my stomach. If they hesitated for even a second, I'd just grab their hands and move 'em across my huge stomach like it was a damn Ouija board. Sometimes they screamed (or tried to spell out HELP ME), but I let them go eventually.

I get that you think it's rude for strangers to touch your tummy, but here's why you're wrong: The very second that baby bolts out of your "down there" and into the world, you are—trust me—No Longer Special. Now the baby will get all the attention, and you? You're yesterday's news, condemned to sit around lactating nonstop, throwing Munchkins at *A Baby Story* every time it comes on, and wondering why you were so hateful to all those well-meaning strangers in the grocery store. You were a rock star, and now? Not so much. Yes, it's invasive and a bit ham-handed, but people feel oddly connected to something greater than themselves when they touch a pregnant woman's tummy.

Get over yourself and enjoy the attention. This is the only time in your life when other women will not only let you cut the line in the ladies' room, but they'll even smile while they're doing it. Good with the bad, honey; good with the bad.

Question: My baby is only a few days old, and I can't figure out a polite way to ask people to please wash

***their hands or use hand sanitizer before they touch
her. Am I being overly protective?***

Not at all. I was so germ conscious when the Princess was
born that I didn't take her out of the house for four weeks.
Friends would joke that they had to visit her like she was roy-
alty: They would drive up, and I would hold her up in the living room window for them to admire, and then I would make
her fat little arm wave "bye-bye!"

My friend Pam was an exception because, even as she visited us in the hospital, she immediately walked over to the
sink and washed her hands like she was going into surgery. I
loved her for that and I still do.

These days, hand sanitizer is ubiquitous, which is Latin for
"every damn where." Just smile as nicely as you can and ask
that they use it or wash their hands. Here's the deal: You're
now in charge of a defenseless infant's health and welfare.
Do you really give much of a shit about hurting someone's
feelings when your kid's health could be at stake? I sincerely
hope not.

Please take this opportunity to ask visitors to leave their
toddlers at home or at least keep them away from your newborn. Toddlers are germ factories, and they love nothing
more than licking babies on the face. It's weird as hell, but
they can't seem to help themselves. Keep them away. If the
toddler in question happens to be a sibling, you might want

to consider establishing a separate residence for that first year. Kidding! Eight months is long enough for the baby's antibodies to kick in.

Question: My friends want to have a baby shower for my third child. I appreciate their generosity, but I'm afraid it will make me look greedy. I've already had two babies and two showers.

Your instincts are right. You don't want to be that person whom people remember as "you know, the one who had, like, a zillion baby showers. I went broke buying crap for her kids."

The first shower—with its goofy games, bow hats, and the rest—is a wonderful tradition. The second one, if you're sure the baby's sex is going to be different, is fine, too. You can't very well expect your baby daughter to wear those Thomas the Tank Engine overalls with the sweet potato stains on them, can you? Or vice versa, the Cinderella Onesies on your new baby boy.

But a third shower? Uhhhh, no. Thank these wannabe hostesses effusively but explain that you're all set. If they persist, or act as if they will physically keel over and die if they don't get to buy something presh for the baby, ask them to buy it and donate it to a baby charity in honor of your newborn. Simple, classy, done.

Question: People keep telling me that they know I'm having a girl (or a boy) because I'm carrying high, look the same from the back as I always did, et cetera, et cetera. I'm weary of all this folk "wisdom." How can I get them to stop?

Guessing the sex of the baby has always been a hot topic, particularly among coworkers. I can tell you one thing with absolute certainty. The baby you have will be a boy. Or a girl. Oh, let them prattle on about it; it doesn't hurt. When I was pregnant, someone dangled a wedding ring on a string over my belly and pronounced I was having a boy. Dumbass.

Question: The other day, I asked a woman when she was due, and she bristled and informed me that she wasn't pregnant. I immediately apologized, but I'm just so mortified that I can't stop thinking about my rude mistake.

I know exactly how you feel. Sometimes a good old-fashioned cirrhotic liver can precisely duplicate the look of pregnancy. I suggest that you start off slow if you must discuss these things with a stranger. Try: "I'm sorry, but are you pregnant or is that a cirrhotic liver I see before me?"

Kidding! Never, ever ask a woman if she's pregnant. As

you found out the hard way, there's just no telling sometimes whether you're looking at a precious bundle of joy or a booze-soaked swollen organ. It's a crapshoot, so just keep your trap shut.

Question: Everybody calls my little boy a girl! I can't tell you how many times this happens when we're out running errands. How can I set them straight?

There are few of us who haven't confused a baby boy with a baby girl at some point in our cooing over a cute infant. Frankly, it's your fault for not dressing your child in obvious gender-specific clothing. Perhaps you subscribe to the notion that gender shouldn't be important. I read recently about a couple who refused to tell anyone—even the grandparents!—whether their toddler was a boy or a girl. I like to call these parents morons.

Now seems like a good time to point out this trend of not cutting a little boy's hair even as it falls below his shoulders is frankly tiresome. Oh, if I saw one more picture of Kate Hudson toting that boy-child of hers with his tangled hair streaming down his tiny back . . . The kids always look unkempt and kind of like Cousin Itt from *The Addams Family.* If that's the look you're going for, well, Godspeed. It's different for girls, of course, because there are so many darling ways to decorate that long hair (bows, braids, barrettes, bandeaus) and keep it out of eyes and face. Not so with boys, who all just look like Mowgli.

Question: At a family reunion recently, a distant cousin asked me if I was breastfeeding my newborn! Is that really any of her business?

Oh, she's just making conversation, and once she got past the obligatory, "Wow! I can't believe how good Gran looks!" or "This is the best pimento cheese I've ever eaten!" your breasts are pretty much third in line. I'll admit that the question is intrusive and you would be within your rights to say, "Why do you ask?" which will make her sputter a bit. She has no idea why she asked, except you've always made her nervous and insecure because your family had an in-ground pool and hers had to be content with one of those ghastly aboveground metal ones where the sides bolt together. I'm just guessing, of course. It's not like that sort of thing ever happened in my life.

Laugh gently and say, "What a question!" Frankly, I'm wondering where she's headed with this. Is there a follow-up question brewing? ("'Cause I was just thinking, if you're not gonna pump for a while, could my kids stand under those things for shade? It's mighty hot out here.")

Question: My baby shower wasn't much fun, because everyone insisted on giving me their own horror stories

of long labors, missed opportunities for epidurals, emergency C-sections, and the like. Why can't people understand that I don't want or need to hear all that negative stuff? I'm nervous enough as it is!

I know, but we can't help ourselves. You're probably recognizing a trend in my responses. While all these issues could be construed as nosy and rude, I tend to keep it real in matters maternal. Don't you think that cavewomen did the same thing? One sympathetically patting the other's hairy hand and grunting about her fifty-six-hour labor with only a cool leaf to chew on? Childbirth is exceedingly personal, but it bonds us together like nothing else.

Of course, if you have a friend who insists on only concentrating on the icky stuff ("You know, inverted-nipple syndrome is more common than you'd think!"), you are welcome to feign tiredness and ask her to give you some nap time.

Let these women into your life, though. Because there's a very good chance that, along with the horror stories, they're carrying a casserole and a nice salad for dinner.

Question: I was strolling my toddler the other day, and a stranger told me that she hoped I had applied sunscreen and then she said it was really the wrong time of day to be out for a stroll, considering the sun's

**strength, and so on. Why do people think they can talk
to me like this?**

It's vexing, I know. You expect to hear that kind of nagging
from your family members but not from complete strangers.
I'll just have to assume that your kid's cheeks look like a ba-
boon's hindparts and the stranger is genuinely concerned.

Be prepared to absorb all sorts of unsolicited advice when
you are raising a child. Usually it's completely well inten-
tioned and can actually prove useful; the best brand of dia-
per rash ointment, the store with the best prices on your
favorite diapers, the best all-night pharmacy in your town . . .
that's helpful information, but it can sound rather high-handed
if you let it. Don't. This is just the way it works. And one day, it
might be you cautioning a young mother that her toddler is
playing with a stick that will most assuredly put his eye out.

Admit it: You also never thought you'd be that person
sitting in a restaurant at Disney World who suddenly smells
something icky, grabs her baby, and presses her nose to his
bottom, inhaling like it's blow. But there you are. Mercifully,
butt-sniffing in public is given a pass when it's a baby. Etiquette understands that sometimes instinct takes over. If,
however, your instinct also tells you to change the baby at the
table, ignore it. That's just gross.

chapter 7

PDAs:
His Hand, Her Crack . . .
Must Be Love

My dear friend David High shares my distaste for public displays of affection to the extent that he alerts me, via e-mail from his home near Nashville, whenever he sees a particularly heinous offense.

So I wasn't surprised when I heard from him recently with this cryptic pronouncement:

> At the mall. Two 16-year-olds. She already has a muffin top, he has a wisp of a mustache, and they're walking along, each with a hand tucked down deep inside the other's waistband.

Oh, my.

David calls this "walking tacky," and as you know, "tacky"

is the worst thing anybody can ever say about anybody else in the Southland. (He also considers it "riding tacky" when you see the couple jammed together in the front seat of a car, and, as always, I agree.)

Public displays of affection are a serious breach of etiquette. Affection should be private and "displayed" only between seriously committed romantic couples during the magic window just after *The Daily Show* is over and just before you realize it's too late for anything but that recurring dream about Matthew McConaughey winning an Academy Award for best actor and thanking you for being there for him every step of the way, "darlin'." Kidding! He could never win an Oscar.

PDAs, including the type David had the misfortune to witness (and, really, are they going to eat orange chicken in the food court with those hands?), seem to be on the rise.

The other day, I arrived a few minutes early to pick up the Princess from a club meeting at her high school. I assumed the early pickup position, reading her dog-eared *Seventeen* magazine while half-listening to public radio discuss Syrian warlords (I am nothing if not well rounded), when what to my wondering eyes should appear . . .

A couple, both about sixteen, sitting across the quad, locked in a public amorous display, that's what. She was straddling him and giving him a tongue-ectomy. He had his hands under her T-shirt. I quickly lost all interest in both "how to rock the perfect smoky eye!" and Syria. Copulating, or mighty close to it, on a concrete bench on the front lawn of a public high school on a main highway? That's so Raven. No, what I meant to say was "Ick!"

I resisted the urge to spring from my car and douse them both with the remains of my Vitamin Water. But this isn't like breaking up a spat on the elementary school playground. This is a playground of an entirely different sort.

Mercifully, the Princess arrived just as I was pondering my next move.

"Did you see that?" I said, jerking my head in the direction of the couple, which was now reenacting the cover of *The Notebook* as a light drizzle failed to preempt their passion.

"Oh, yeah," she said. "They always do that."

This is what we parents like to call a Teachable-Ass Moment.

"You wouldn't act like that in public, would you?" I asked.

Eye roll, followed by immediate installation of earbuds. Conversation over.

Well. I think I made my point.

Question: My girlfriend likes to talk baby talk to me when we're alone, which is okay, I guess, but she also does it in front of my friends. We're both in our early twenties, and I'm embarrassed by the way she talks to me in public. How can I get her to stop?

You can't. You can only break up with her in a note signed: *No longer your "Snookums Pootie Bear."*

Just as an animal marks its territory, your girlfriend is metaphorically circling and spraying around you, signaling to your friends, whom she probably detests, that you have a bond that can't be broken. That she is your widdle wuvver-dover and they better back the shit off. She knows it irritates you, but it's more important that she show your friends that she's the one in control. Simply put: She has infantilized you, and now you must cut the cord. Put it to her in terms she'll understand: "We're overkins."

Question: My husband always gives me flowers on Valentine's Day, my birthday, and our anniversary. This is very nice of him, but I have asked him time and time again to have them sent to my office instead of just bringing them home to me. Everyone knows it doesn't count unless your coworkers see what a great guy he is and how much he loves you.

I know that what you have written—in excruciating detail, I might add—is incredibly shallow, but I have to agree. It's like the old "If a tree falls in the forest and nobody hears it, did it make a sound?" Or, to put it another way, "If your husband brings you flowers at home and nobody saw them, was his money wasted?"

I don't know jack shit about the tree/forest thing, but I can say, without hesitation, that flowers brought home for special occasions do not count. Also, there's a better-than-average chance that he bought them at the grocery store instead of the florist. He's saving a ton on delivery charges, which, frankly, shows you where you stand. The presentation of flowers at your workplace is a public display of affection that is to be encouraged. Cheaping out on flowers by buying them from someone who also slices sausage by the pound is not.

Question: My boyfriend and I are in our late twenties, and have been dating for two years. Whenever we go out, if there's any kind of a wait, he likes to pass the time by making out. I'm embarrassed by the way people look at us, all the pointing, snickering, and the inevitable suggestion that we "get a room." How can I get him to understand that this is not something I'm comfortable doing?

Truthfully, I just can't relate. At this stage in my own courtship with Duh Hubby, he would be overjoyed at the mention of a wait as long as there was a bar with the game (any game) on. We would spend the entire wait watching the game, drinking a couple of "foamers," and then our names would be called. Your old-enough-to-know-better boyfriend sounds like someone who likes showing off his horn-dog behavior for an audience. It's a little creepy. Normal guys just don't act like that. And, yes, I'm sure you're very alluring, but, really, the bloom should be off the rose by now. I'm presuming that you've mentioned that you don't like this and he just isn't listening. If you stay with him, you can be sure he won't listen to anything else that matters to you either. He's an asshat; dump him.

Question: My boyfriend and I are one of those couples that find it exciting to make out in public. We're both on the same page about this, so, really, what's the big deal?

Get back to class. The bell's getting ready to ring.

Acceptable PDAs . . .

- Hand-holding.
- Arm looped around the shoulder.
- Quick kiss on lips or cheek to greet SO. (No tongue!)

Nonacceptable PDAs . . .

- Everything not listed above.

Nonromantic PDAs . . .

When we talk about PDAs, we usually connect it to romantic love or just outright gotta-hit-that lust, but there's another kind of PDA that is just plain weird and offensive. I speak, of course, of the chalk drawings on the rear window of the minivan you're behind in traffic.

What more public display of affection than a groovy little height-ordered depiction of all your loved ones? There's Dad, looking tall and in control, even as a chalk outline. There's Mom, fuzzy haired and goofy in her mom-skirt. There are the kids and even the family dog, cat, and *bird*.

I get that this is meant to tell the world that You Love Your Family. But, if we're being honest, the subtext in this particular and very public display of affection is that My Family Is Probably Better Than Yours. (P.S. Did you not see our *bird*?)

Question: What's so bad about letting the world know that you love your family? You make it sound as if that's a bad thing.

First of all, you're not letting the "world" know anything, unless you honestly think the world begins and ends at the exact route that takes you from school to gymnastics to choir practice to ballet to the grocery store. Scary how well I know your pathetic little routine, isn't it? Why, it's almost as if it's my routine, too. Because it is. And that's my point: There's nothing special about your family. You love them and that's as it should be, but pasting scary, emaciated decals of them on the back of your car doesn't make them better than my family or anybody else's. Quit boasting about your brood, or I'll be tempted to show you a bird of my own next time we meet on the way to the PTA meeting. Where worlds collide.

Question: I'm considering getting a tattoo of my dead (brother, cousin, mother, NASCAR hero, sister, aunt, father, coon dog . . .) as a way of letting the world know how much they meant to me. Then, when that's done, I'm going to get a decal on my truck's rear window that says in really big letters: RIP *with their name and birth and death dates. What do you think? Isn't that a fantastic tribute?*

Oh, sorry. My skin just crawled a little. What were you saying? Oh, heavenly Lord, why must you force your undoubtedly sincere and heartfelt grief on an unsuspecting public?

I don't mean to be cruel, here, but if I'm out on the town with my gal pals and we get behind one more giant RIP JUAN . . . 1984-2011 complete with a semi-artistic rendering of Juan and his little dog, too, I am going to scream, *"Buzzkill!"* out the window just a little too loudly.

Grief is something that has no place on the back window of a truck. At times like this, you should ask yourself WWJD? ("What would Juan do?" naturally.)

Would he really want to bum out 99 percent of the motoring public? I'm guessing not. I didn't know Juan, but I imagine he would be a tad embarrassed by this whole thing.

Grieve privately and with those who actually knew Juan and can share in your grief. Anything else just looks like you're trying to overcompensate. Perhaps you had a hand in Juan's untimely demise? Hmmmm? Frankly, if this were an episode of *Law & Order,* I'd "like" you as the "perp." Think about it. And get that damn thing off the window.

chapter 8

Husbands and Wives:
He May Not Be Much, But He's <u>Your</u>
Tube Sock Filled with Gravy

Perhaps it's because you've seen him trim his toenails in bed over an open copy of *Sports Illustrated* one too many times. Perhaps it's because he's seen you spend a full five minutes pulling up your pantyhose until he finally screamed, *"My eyes!"*

Husbands and wives don't always demonstrate good manners to one another. Familiarity breeds contempt, the saying goes, and it's a damn shame.

Of all the people we encounter who deserve an extra measure of thoughtfulness, our life partner should be first in line. So how is it, then, that you are once again standing in front of the fridge, holding a milk carton that contains exactly one tablespoon of milk?

Basic consideration is all that we ask. Treat us as respectfully as you treat your clients, your boss—hell, the waitress at that Cracker Barrel on the interstate that you will never see again.

Usually, we're equally guilty. Sometimes the slide begins when the kids come. Gone is all pretense that life will ever be the same. The only time he will open that door for you now is if you are toting the infant carrier *and* the porta-crib.

Remember how you used to make his favorite meal? Chicken cordon bleu with wild rice and sautéed spinach? Who has time for that now? Certainly not you. It's almost time for *The Bachelor,* and you've already eaten but there's a can of soup somewhere in the pantry.

Your marital manners matter, my hons. This doesn't mean you have to treat each other like you did when you were dating, but it does mean that you don't completely coast, taking each other for granted.

Question: Whenever my husband sees his ex-wife, he greets her with a big hug even if I'm standing right there! I think this is rude and disrespectful to me. What's wrong with a handshake?

Well, while I agree that a "big hug" seems inappropriate, I don't care for a handshake either. Handshakes are for new acquaintances or the workplace, not for someone who has seen you nekkid and knows that you prefer Astroglide to K-Y

Liquibeads. It would be weird. That said, I think you should tell your husband that a cheerful "Hi, how are you doing?" is quite enough. If she looks puzzled and reaches out to hug him, you would be within your rights to kick her ass.

Question: My wife still has the wedding album from her first marriage. I know it shouldn't bother me, but it does. Would it be bad manners of me to ask her to throw it away?

Presuming that she doesn't have it displayed on your coffee table with lighted candles flanking either side, I don't think you should ask her to destroy it. There are many reasons that women (and some men) keep their wedding albums, and it is no reflection on your current relationship. I, for instance, have the album from my first marriage, which was a tidy little six-year, no-kids matter that ended semi-amicably. I keep the album in my attic for one reason: That wedding cost my parents a shitload of money. No, that's not entirely true. I keep it because it contains possibly the best picture of me that has ever been taken under any circumstances. My wedding portrait from that ill-fated "starter" marriage made me look like Charlize Theron, only much younger and prettier. And, yes, bitches, it was retouched from now till Tuesday, but so what? In every picture, I am glowing and Charlizing all over the place.

Trust me: Keeping the old wedding album doesn't diminish for a second what you have now with your wife. She, like many of us, just likes to remember what it felt like to be a silken-skinned goddess, if only for a day.

Question: My husband went to Duke, and I went to Carolina. Needless to say, game nights are very intense and unpleasant around our house. When Duke gets behind, he yells, assumes a ferretlike countenance, and slaps the floor with both hands just like the Duke players. His rudeness is making it impossible to savor the game. If Duke loses, he pouts for days. Like a little girl. Do you think we should just stop watching games together?

No, I don't. I happen to think that watching sports together can be one of the most mutually satisfying elements of a happy marriage.

You can certainly have a successful "mixed" marriage; many couples do. *But,* before you marry, make sure you have a similar level of commitment to the concept of rivalry. I remember my precious Duh Hubby being dismayed at a friend's comment to her husband following a tournament game.

"Did you hear her?" he asked me, incredulous. "She said that if Carolina lost, she'd still pull for Duke because the important thing is that an ACC team advances."

This sort of Ned Flanders piffle is simply unacceptable. True Duke fans don't pull for UNC and vice versa. I don't care if your granny's been on a vent at Duke for six years and you bring the nurses Chick-fil-A every second Thursday, you don't pull for Duke if you like UNC. Ever. What I'm saying is that things aren't as bad as you think. Better to be married to a committed fan than a wishy-washy one because he will probably feel just as passionately about sticking with you. Sure, it's nice when you root for the same team, but you knew your husband's Serious Flaw when you married him, so stop whining.

Question: Why can't my husband be more sensitive? We started a diet together on New Year's Day, and he's lost fifteen pounds to my four. I know he's worked harder, but he rudely insists on telling everyone about our little contest and how much better he's doing. How can I get him to stop?

I'd tell you how to lose 205 pounds overnight, but that involves getting a divorce, which, I'll agree, is a bit extreme. Duh and I are often on one diet or the other. And, yes, he has done much better than I, owing to his inclusion of "exercise" and "strength conditioning" and "flexibility workouts." This is in direct opposition to my plan, which includes "sitting on my ass" "eight to twelve hours a day" "okay, more like sixteen."

What can I tell you? Some words just don't go together in my world. Words like "exercise" and "happiness" or "library" and "Kardashian."

We have even had weekly weigh-ins—a terrible idea, by the way. Duh weighs with all his clothes on. I, on the other hand, will go so far as to floss before stepping on the scales. The last time, he chuckled and said flossing wouldn't affect the weight unless "you're planning to pull a tractor tire outta there!" Right. So where do I get one of those again?

But I digress. This is extremely rude behavior on your husband's part and an excellent example of what I was talking about earlier: showing your life partner an even greater measure of thoughtfulness. Your husband should be your greatest champion, not tearing you down for laughs in front of your friends. Tell him so, tubby.

Question: I can't believe you just said that to her.

Oh, settle down. It's just to make a point. Sometimes we women can be a bit hypersensitive. I once heard Duh tell a friend his gut looked like a tube sock filled with gravy, and the guy just laughed. Maybe we should lighten up a bit.

Question: My husband never dresses up anymore. Even to go out to dinner with friends, he'll just put on his jeans and a T-shirt that says I'M WHAT WILLIS WAS

TALKIN' 'BOUT or something equally stupid. Isn't this disrespectful to me?

Not really. I know you don't want him to wear it to a wedding, but "disrespectful" is a tad harsh. It's not like he took a poo on your head. A T-shirt that evokes warm memories of a better-than-average '70s/'80s sitcom isn't the worst thing in the world. Look, most men will just wear whatever is closest to them. If you want him to dress up a bit, just drop the clothes you'd like him to wear on the floor beside the bed or, if he's showering, on the bathroom floor. He'll put them on because they're there. Problem solved.

Question: My husband leaves razor stubble in the sink. This is the grossest, rudest thing I can imagine. I've asked him to stop leaving his tiny hairs all over the sink, but he always forgets.

While I'm no fan of the stubble in the sink, I think he's probably just as grossed out by those random long hairs that cling to the shower curtain, the shower stall walls, and, of course, the tub drain. Did you ever think about that, Rapunzel?

Also, if those tiny bits of beard are the "grossest, rudest thing" you can imagine, you have clearly never watched *The Human Centipede*. Check it out and get back to me. As for a practical solution that takes about ten seconds, two words: Clorox Wipes. Tell him to swipe one into the sink after shaving and vow to do the same after you shampoo. Now, has anybody got a *real* problem for me?

Question: I've told my husband that it's bad manners to walk around the house wearing only his underwear. What do you think?

Really. Anyone at all. A *Real* problem?

Question: We also fight about money a lot. Sometimes in front of the kids. Oh, and we never have sex anymore. Oh, and . . .

Ding-ding-ding! You have my attention. Don't fight in front of your cherubs; that's the height of rudeness. Plus you'll screw 'em up and they'll end up like poor Chaz Bono, going on talk shows and telling everybody how he's going to buy himself a tallywacker for Christmas. Don't say I didn't warn you.

chapter 9

*

Waiting Game:
How to Deal with Line-Jumpers and
Other Creeps of Nature

One of my favorite recurring skits on *Saturday Night Live* features the "Two A-Holes." They're married to each other, or at least in some sort of relationship. She is brilliantly played by a blond-wigged Kristen Wiig wearing stilettos, a short, tight skirt, and a perpetually bored expression. He is just as brilliantly played by a be-sweatered, entirely vacant Jason Sudeikis. Both are sadly familiar.

Two A-Holes are shown in a variety of settings acting rude, demanding, and infuriatingly clueless. They're hilarious until you meet them in person, as I did, at that great equalizer of all humanity, the line at the U.S. Post Office and Lunch Hour Detention Center.

With about a dozen people in line behind them, these

Two A-Holes remained oblivious of everyone around them while "She" pondered the available stamp selections, asking which "He" preferred.

"I dunno, babe," he responded. "What do you think?" (OMGod! The *SNL* couple says the same thing! Were there hidden cameras somewhere?)

She kept smacking her gum and flipping back her long blond hair *like it was her job* while we all waited and seethed in silence.

"Baaaaabe," she talk-whined loud enough for all to hear. "Who's Dinah Shore? Huh? Dinah Shore?"

HE:　Huh? Who? I dunno, babe. What about these breast cancer stamps? What about them? Huh, babe?

SHE:　(still smacking and hair-flipping) They cost, like, more than the other stamps, babe. (And to the harried postal clerk who is working alone because, as we all know, the U.S. Postal Service is Very Serious about eating a nutritious lunch at the noon hour every day—) *Why do they gotta cost more?*

This stamp-selection bit went on for longer than it took for me to buy my last car. The best part? When a second postal clerk finally appeared, she sashayed over to his window and asked to buy a money order, thus blocking both lines.

This type of blatant asshattery is a huge breach of waiting-in-line etiquette.

When standing in line, most of us realize that We Are All in This Together, so there's a general vibe that you don't screw it up for everybody else if you can help it.

It is highly recommended and encouraged that, if you encounter this sort of rudeness, you may roll your eyes, sigh very heavily and frequently, mutter things like "Christ on a cracker, wouldja get on with it already!" and, finally, as I did recently, just let it all out there and say in a loud, firm voice: *"Move!"*

Yeah, I did.

It's funny how people look at you like you're the crazy one when you do something like that.

Like asking somebody when you first meet them, "Hey, how much money do you make?" it's just completely unexpected.

"Move!" A one-word sentence that conveys the absolute frustration and borderline homicidal rage you're feeling will yield immediate results.

So shocked by what I did, the offender did, in fact, move. Sometimes, etiquette demands that you fall on the metaphorical sword for everyone in line behind you. I was fairly hoisted upon everyone's shoulders like that little kid in the Old El Paso taco shell commercial when I said *"Move!"*

I could feel the love of everyone in the line behind me. I had given voice to the voiceless, and hell, maybe I'd get my own stamp along with Dinah Shore, whoever the hell that was.

Question: I've been the victim of line-jumping. What is an appropriate response to this sort of rude behavior?

Ah, yes. The line-jumper. I've seen this in venues as diverse as the line at the K&W Cafeteria (a Southern staple also rather uncharitably known as "Canes & Wheelchairs" because of its elderly clientele) and the line to the T-shirt concession at a Mumford & Sons concert.

Usually, line-jumpers wave very energetically at someone they know who is waaaaaay up in the line, practically at the congealed lime Jell-O with pears if you're at K&W. (I've always thought the pears look a little trapped in that gelatin, like they're screaming to get out. . . .) The fruit salad, as everyone knows, is the real starting point once you get your tray and cutlery from the beefy guy who has GOOD and EVIL tatted on his knuckles and is wearing a hairnet. (As an aside: You no longer look badass when you're wearing a hairnet; trust moi.)

At the concert, it was the same. Silly young woman waving semi-hysterically to real or imagined friends at the front of the line. Fortunately, I didn't have to handle this one on my own. She was told by a guy wearing an I DIRECT MIDGET PORN T-shirt that she needed to get to the back of the line where she belonged.

Well played, sir.

So, the answer is you stand up for what's right and you

politely and firmly tell the offender to retreat. Sometimes, if you're not lucky enough to have a midget porn director in your corner, there will be pouting and pleading. Do not fall for it. If homegirl wanted to get in the front of the line, she should've spent less time on her stupid crackle nail polish and headed her scrawny ass down to the concert in a timely fashion.

And just so we're clear—crackle nail polish? Ick.

Question: What do you make of those people who act all surprised when it's time to pay up and start fumbling for their wallets/checkbooks/debit cards only at the end of the transaction, thus making everyone in line wait even longer?

Ha! That's an easy one. Those people need to spend the rest of eternity encased between New Jersey Governor Chris Christie's ass cheeks. Well. You asked.

These people hold up the line for the selfsame reason a dog licks his naughties or a Republican votes against preschool programs for poor kids: because it just feels so darned good!

They know exactly what they're doing as they blissfully ignore the world around them until the cashier asks for payment. It's the one time of the day when they can experience a heady sense of power over others. Every movement is excruciating. Reaching into pocket or fumbling for purse. It's just all going to take such a long time. Never mind that, if this takes place in a grocery store, half the line has given up and retreated to the vile U-Scans, where they think they have a little more control. Of course, everyone knows that these are actually slower because with every scan, there's the "Wait for attendant!" command.

Here's some good news, though: Thanks to the Internet, waiting in line could become a relic of the past, like Heather Locklear. No, really. You can order your groceries online and either pick 'em up, ready to go, or have them delivered. Ahhhh.

You can order stamps online and even get a gizmo that weighs your packages and affixes proper postage. Ahhhhh-hhh.

And you can order concert tickets that will allow you to print out a ticket that, okay, entitles you to stand in the Will Call line, so, uh, maybe that wasn't such a great example.

But you get the idea. You could almost say that, by the time you read this, the only reason anyone, anywhere should be standing in a line is in a fast-food situation.

They really haven't figured out a way to make your computer printer spit out a gordita on command, so your fat ass will still have to queue up at Taco Bell every so often. So will my fat ass. And, very possibly, Chris Christie's fat ass. With all those people in it.

Think about it.

Of course, some lines are inevitable and it always makes me weep with appreciation when there is recognition that people hate lines and deserve a little extra sumpin'-sumpin' when they are forced to endure one. Like how when you're in line for a table at Outback Steakhouse and they send out the chick with a tray of Bloomin Onion bits and ranch sauce just to tide you over. Now *that*'s respecting the agony that is waiting in line.

Universal Studios also recognizes line hell, and they have misters that keep you cool and delightfully moist while you wait. How thoughtful!

Why can't the post office send out a nice man with free stamps or packing tape samples when this sort of thing occurs? People, I've experienced check-in at O'Hare International Airport, so I know just how long a line can be. It is a documented fact that the distance between check-in and security is roughly 46.8 miles at O'Hare. Soooo, why can't they send out an airline representative who will take over the job of kicking your bag ahead a few feet at a time just so you won't have to. He could work the whole line, kicking everbody's triflin' luggage.

Imagine how much we'd all enjoy that sort of acknowledgment.

The High Points and Some Real-Life Tips . . .

You all know that long lines provoke rude behavior, so take steps to avoid them in the first place.

How do you do that? Easy. Just do your business at a time of day when nobody else is going to be around. This may sound painfully obvious, but it works. For instance, sure, you like to handle your package-mailing and the like at lunch hour because that's the only time you have all day to do it. Why not go at midnight and use the convenient auto-system in the lobby? You can weigh packages, buy stamps, and do just about everything you need to with a single swipe of your credit card. Nobody will be there at that hour except the serial rapist. Take pepper spray. He hates that shit.

Don't be a douche. Hold out for the Bloomin Onion even when they bring around the fried mushrooms. It's a trap. Everybody has fried mushrooms. Save your stomach space for the Holy Grail of Apps. You're welcome.

chapter 10

Office Manners:
Loud Talkers, Cake Hawkers, and
Britney Sue's Unfortunate Cyst

These days, I work from home in a tiny Carolina blue–colored office with room for a wraparound desk, two chairs from Staples, a floor-to-ceiling bookcase, and not much else. I'm lucky to have three windows in this upstairs room, so the light floods in pretty much all day. My only companion, for hours on end, is the squirrel who moved into our attic this winter and spends his days noisily shelling pecans over my head. I've named him Antonio for no particular reason. People who work from home and don't see or talk to another adult for hours at a time tend to do crazy shit like naming invisible rodents.

Although I work from home now, I spent many years in a real office, complete with shared coffeepot, slanderous gossip, a coworker who wore a gagsome amount of Estée Lauder Beautiful, and a boss with a split personality who left me feeling like his adored daughter one moment and something on the bottom of his shoe the next.

There are times, honestly, when I miss the office banter and even the schitzy boss. Face it; it's hard to stay motivated when you work from home and there are all those Netflixed episodes of (wait for it) *How I Met Your Mother* just twenty feet away, calling my name.

But that's a "me problem," and we will now concern ourselves with real office etiquette, which—from what I can tell from interviewing my friends in the working world—is getting worse all the time. . . .

Question: My company is downsizing because of the lousy economy, and one of my favorite coworkers just got laid off. I feel terrible for her. What's the correct etiquette on letting her know how sorry I am?

Admit it. You're sorry she got the ax, but you're relieved as hell that it wasn't you. Understandable. In this economy, it's not unusual to arrive at work and be told you're no longer needed by the time you unpack your lunch. It happened to my sister, who was laid off recently after twenty-seven years at the same job. She was fired by a dreadful troll of a man who had been on the job for eight months and who immediately installed a much younger woman with virtually no experience in my sister's job and gave himself a twelve-thousand-dollar pay raise.

I believe "asswipe" covers it nicely.

Wait. We were talking about you, weren't we? It's just that when you witness such acute douchery up close and personal, it shakes you to the core. But, to answer your question, the only tactful thing to do is say, "I'm so sorry." Don't say, "This place sucks and I can't wait to get outta here myself." That's condescending and doesn't make her feel any better. You should follow up by arranging a get-together (think frothy rum drinks at Applebee's) with like-minded coworkers. This will cheer her a bit, and you can bash the boss for a few hours in relative peace and quiet because, let's face it, nobody goes to Applebee's.

Question: A coworker routinely places his lunch leftovers in the office fridge and leaves them there for days, even weeks. It's not my job to clean up after this slob, but if I don't do it, the break room simply reeks. What should I do?

I'm assuming that, like Randy Quaid's daughter in *National Lampoon's Vacation,* you were, sadly, born without a tongue. I assume this because I can't imagine a grown-up-type person not simply calling out this boor. Most of the time, in my experience, the offender has simply forgotten about the leftovers. You shouldn't clean up behind him; you should stand there, arms folded, tapping your foot and pursing your lips while you watch *him* toss the smelly reekage from the fridge. It can become your Friday routine, along with weekend nails and waiting for your married boyfriend to call.

Question: How did you know that I have a married boyfriend?!

I'm crazy smart that way. Also, Antonio told me. He reads minds, you know. Shit, I might need to get out of here more often....

Question: A woman in our office keeps a calendar with all our birthdays marked on it. She then takes up money and buys a cake so we can celebrate. We hate her and want her to stop because nobody needs that much cake, it's a creepy forced kind of friendliness,* and *we think she pockets at least an extra ten bucks every time, because she usually buys marked-down cakes from the grocery store freezer.

Oh, the cake monster. There's one in every office. She's usually middle-aged, smells vaguely of litter box, and has hair just like the mom in *That '70s Show*.

Of course, she's working a cake scam. It's one of the oldest cons in the workplace, along with the "Susan's aunt/grandma/

mother-in-law died, and we're taking up money for flowers. . . ."
I'll bet she bought new drapes from Pier 1 with the extras
from her cake-extortion fund. And, oh, how Fluffy does love
to climb them!

The solution is easy. Tell Cake Monster that you've taken a
poll and people are concerned about expanding waistlines
and midafternoon consumption of empty calories. In other
words, the party's over.

It's okay, by the way, to solicit money for ailing coworkers
who are legitimately in the hospital or recuperating at home.
My Duh Hubby warmly remembers working at the Thomas
Built school bus factory while in college and being asked to
give a dollar to Britney Sue's flower fund.

When he innocently asked what had happened to Britney
Sue, he was told by the gruff foreman shaking the cash-filled
pickle jar in front of him: "Britney Sue had a cyst on her pussy."

"Put me down for two," said Duh.

Eat your hearts out, ladies.

*Question: A colleague who works six cubicles over has
such a loud phone voice! I can hear every word he's
saying all day long. Sometimes it's business; sometimes it's not. How can I politely ask him to lower his
voice? All of us are bothered by this.*

I'm assuming that "all of us" doesn't include your boss or
the folks in Human Resources. They don't know a thing about

it because you are all acting like a bunch of lady parts that are prone to cysts. Just sayin'.

This fella probably doesn't even know that he's a loud talker, so he's not doing it to be rude. So tell him. Use your words. Say: "You have a very booming voice, and I don't think you realize that we can all hear every word you're saying. Could you please lower your voice?"

You should be prepared for an immediate apology and even a little embarrassment on his part. You should also be prepared for a very quiet afternoon followed, the next day, by the same loud voice you despise. He has already forgotten. This will necessitate a second visit and perhaps a third and fourth. Retraining loud talkers isn't easy, but it is possible with daily, consistent reminders. Eventually he'll get the hang of it, and harmony will reign. Either that, or it's back to Applebee's for drinks again because his loud ass needs firing.

Question: One of my coworkers believes that the best way to get a promotion is to kiss the boss's ass all day long. What do you think of that strategy?

Sorry. My mouth was full. What did you just ask? I think it's a great strategy, and I'm always surprised that more people don't do it. Don't whine about missed promotions if you're not willing to get in there and really kiss that ass but good! Nobody will respect you, but what do you care? You and the boss are hitting the links this weekend. And you're gonna let him win despite the fact that you had a full ride at Dartmouth on a golf scholarship. He really has a fantastic swing, doesn't he? What part of "floundering economy" do you not get? You can enjoy your lousy principles all the way to the unemployment line. Pucker up!

Question: You know that expression "prairie dogging"? I hate it when people pop their heads up over my cubicle instead of just walking around. It's so, I don't know, invasive.

You know that expression "Grow a pair"? I mean what are you doing in your cubicle that's so damn private anyway? Oh, right. Porn. Cubicles are an unfortunate reality of corporate office design, and short of going all Old Spice guy and hoisting a duffel bag over your shoulders and wandering into the mist to look for work on the docks, you're outta luck.

Question: My office mates often borrow my desk supplies, even taking my stapler and Post-it notes from my desk drawers. It would be okay if they'd ever return them without me nagging. What to do?

Use locks, if you must, because I'll agree that this is extremely rude. No one should be rooting around in anyone else's drawers.

Question: I hate staff meetings, and my company is obsessed with them. We could accomplish so much more by sending concise e-mails to update/explain company business. The worst are the ones where the employee reads every word of a PowerPoint to us while we stare at the screen.

I feel your pain. PowerPoints, poorly done, are toxic to a productive work environment. There is nothing more snooze-inducing than hearing a dronelike recitation of a script that's right in front of you. Okay, I meant except for Nicolas Cage movies. Those are totally worse. I also sympathize with your take on too many meetings. What's the point of having office e-mail if you are going to be dragged into a room filled with bad coffee and vile pastries and detained there for upwards of an hour to rehash something that could've been tackled in less than thirty seconds electronically?

You know what? The more I think about this whole workplace thing, the more I'm realizing that it's pretty sweet to be here with Antonio day after day after day. I don't call any meetings and force myself to attend. I don't have to deal with cake monsters or office supply theft or a public discussion of an eruption on my vagina à la the unfortunate Britney Sue.

Yes, working from home has definite advantages. If something reeks around here, it's me—and I simply send myself a sternly worded e-mail to not let it happen again.

If I continue to mess up, I'll give myself three warnings and then, finally, fire myself. Afterwards, I will take myself to (where else?) Applebee's, where I will spend the afternoon sipping sugary daiquiris surrounded by the car salesmen from the dealership across the street who haven't sold anything since 2009, bless their hearts.

I just wish Antonio could come, but I'm pretty sure they have a no-rodent policy. Pretty sure.

chapter 11

Mom to Mom:
It's Complicated

Face it: It's easier to find Honey Boo Boo's kin on the Mensa membership roll than to find a mom-friend who sees things exactly the way you do. Sure, we know plenty of playground moms we can share grapes and Goldfish crackers with, but true friends are harder to come by.

Rather, we are thrown together, yoga-pantsed soldiers on a brightly colored battlefield who bond only on one thing: Our children are the very best kids on earth. Hell, we feel sorry for all the rest. Tra-la-la!

Actually, I was just thinking about my kid when I said that. Yours are just okay. I mean, the whole endless snot thing that *you refuse to acknowledge* is a bit of a deal-breaker for life-long bonds being forged. Criminy, get some antibiotics, would you?

But every now and then, a true friendship will shine like a

jewel in a goat's ass, and you realize that *this* playground mom is going to be a Forever Friend. You'll probably even take couple's vacations together, your daughter might marry her son, oh! The possibilities are endless.

And then she says it one day as you watch the future bridal couple play with the big yellow tic-tac-toe game painted on the side of the twisty slide: "Hey, you know I think Rush Limbaugh has some great ideas!"

And we're done here. Juicy Juice is packed up, pretzels are resealed in their snack-size ziplock bags, and we really have to wash our hair. You never liked her that much anyway. Oh, and the marriage is *off*!

It's so hard to find the right mom friend from a pool of women who simply have kids the exact same age. Thank the sweet Lord above, I was lucky enough to find several, and fourteen years later, we still get together at least once a month for dinner, drinks, and catch-up.

But there were so many more where the convo was forced, brittle even, as we discovered that, although our kids were crazy about one another, we just didn't click.

It took me quite a while to realize that I didn't have to be BFFs with every other mom. There was no reason to assume that just because we'd given birth within eight months of one another that we had anything else in common.

Be prepared to attend a lot of birthday parties where your kids have a blast playing together while you watch with a big fake smile on your face. The important thing to remember during these forced social situations is that it's not about the parents; it's about the kids. Still, it would be ever so much more convenient if you wouldn't be such an insufferable bitch most of the time.

Question: You know what I hate? When another mom says, "Oh, call me for a playdate with little Madeleine!" That puts the onus on me to call her. That also tells me she doesn't really want a playdate but just wants to look like she does, am I right?

Sadly, yes. No one should ever say "call me" about anything, because it's automatically transferring the obligation to *you,* and that's bad manners. The truth is, if she really wanted your kids to play together, she'd say: "Bring Tallulah over around four on Wednesday if that's convenient. If not, what would be a good time?"

That's a sincere invitation extended sincerely, complete with specifics and, yet, an allowance for the fact that it might not be a convenient time. Nicely done.

Why is it just so hard for moms to make a plan sometimes? I'd rather stay home with the kid watching Mexican soaps than deal with these indecisive weirdos. They may have been corporate bigwigs in their other lives, but now their brains are mush. To wit:

MOM A: Oh, the kids should get together soon. What are y'all doing Tuesday afternoon? We're going to go to Story Time at the library; want to join us?

MOM B: Sounds great! We'll meet you there!

MOM A: Or we could meet for lunch a little earlier. How about that new Indian restaurant? They have a buffet, and the kids even like it.

MOM B: Oh, I can't. We have an appointment to get her baby sister's ears pierced at Merle Norman that day at noon.

MOM A: (silence)

MOM B: You don't approve, right? You think she's too young, right?

MOM A: Nonsense! I can hardly see the amniotic sac residue on her skin anymore. Whatever. Just the library, then.

MOM B: Well, okay. Listen. I have to drop off some overdue books. Can you give me a few extra minutes to run home and pick 'em up?

MOM A: Of course. Hey! How about I drive you to your house so you can get the books, and then we'll ride together.

MOM B: But will my car seats fit in your car?

MOM A: Hmmm. I'll call my mom and see if I can borrow her van. Gimme a minute. . . . Okay, she

says that's fine but only if we bring her back
something from McDonald's.

MOM B: Do we have time?

MOM A: Sure. Just pick up a salad from the one at the
food court when you're at the mall and bring it
to my mom's house.

MOM B: Oh, no! What about nap time? We forgot about
nap time!

MOM A: Right you are! Okay, get the salad at the mall
after you get the baby's ears pierced—don't
forget the spicy Asian dressing, 'cause she
loves that—drive over to my mom's house,
switch your car seats into her van, and the kids
can sleep on the way to your house to pick up
the overdue books, and then we'll go to the
library.

Exhausted yet?

Moms muddy the water a lot by trying to think of everything and accommodate everyone. Nobody wins. Keep it
simple: "We're going to the library for Story Time after lunch
and nap time. Join us if you can!"

Done. Ahhhhh.

*Question: I'm confused about how to approach a mom
friend who allows her children to call me by my first*

name only. I have taught my kids to always call adults "Mr." or "Ms." (last name). What's your best advice on handling this?

Well, doody. And here I was all set to give you my worst advice. Okay, my best advice isn't the easiest thing, unfortunately. The easiest thing is to make an inflexible decree and stick to it. For example, as a daughter of the South, I was taught to call people "Mr." or "Ms." (first name), which is just a little more personal and friendly but probably a Southern thing. Neither answer is right. You should teach your children to address adults exactly the way that adult in particular wants to be addressed. For example, if the school bus driver likes to be called "Ms. Linda," well, that's what your kids should call her. Adults usually make this clear by introducing themselves to a kid by saying, "I'm Mr. Kevin," or "I'm Mr. Timkin," or if they're a little odd, "I'm Mr. Kevin Timkin, but you can call me 'Dude'."

That said, I sometimes hate what adults ask kids to call them. My friend's kids attend a private school where all the students from kindergarten to eighth grade are told to address their teachers by their first names. I think this sounds ridiculous and fairly disrespectful, but I can't say anything, mostly because the huge stick wedged up my ass has now found its way all the way up to my vocal cords.

I can't help it; it's weird hearing a preteen talk to her teacher like he's her friend who watches *iCarly* with her after school instead of a guy with a Ph.D. in Global Studies from Penn.

Question: I'm fighting with a mom, but our daughters are besties. This makes the drop-offs for playdates very awk. What to do?

Who are you? One of those skanky "Teen Moms" from MTV? For starters, talk like a grown-up. "Besties"? "Awk"? What the hell? Look, the kids didn't get the memo that just because you've had a tiff with this mom, it should destroy their friendship. To put it in terms you can understand: Chillax, h8er. This will totes pass. Obvi.

Question: I have a couple of mom friends who are always bragging about their kids' accomplishments. My daughter makes straight A's and has won a decent number of awards in school and for extracurriculars, but it's not something I talk about, because I know how much I hate it when others brag. On the other hand, I think they think my kid is an underachiever since I never join in the brag-fest, which makes me feel almost disloyal to my kid. What to do?

I know exactly how you feel. While a normal amount of catching up on the kids is great when couples get together, some parents don't know when it ceases to be interesting news and disintegrates into unpleasant bragging and one-upmanship. Susie won the Science Olympiad. Susie got first chair in the all-state symphony. Susie's senior project is to build an affordable assisted-living facility for blind children. Christ, I don't even know her and I'm already sick of this kid.

So you end up swirling your chard a bit too wildly in its glass, dying to say: "Oh, shut *up,* you braggy *cow!* Your kid is about as special as mildew; move on!"

The only thing you can do is change the subject. This isn't disloyal; it's self-preservation. Just as the offending parent is revving up to discuss Susie's athletic prowess (shot put record for the school—seriously?), throw something completely random out there. Say: "You know I read somewhere that people who brag about their kids all the time have very unsatisfying sex lives. Is that true?"

I'm kidding, of course. Although it would definitely be the talk of the Fit 'n' Forty Zumba class at the Y the next day and, therefore, totally worth it.

When tempted to brag about your kid, remember that Karma ain't just a dive bar on the Jersey Shore. Play nice. And keep your mouth shut. At least until the inauguration/Nobel acceptance ceremony/space flight. Then, yeah, you can do the superior dance. But only for a minute.

You don't want to sound like Amy Chua, the now-famous "Tiger Mom." Ever since I read about Chua, I've pictured her oldest daughter scratching rebellious little marks into her bedpost, counting down the days until she can leave for college. You have to feel like a prisoner when your mama won't even let you take a pee break from five hours of violin practice. In my mommy-fantasy world, I'd love to run into Chua's daughter one day, hanging out with the scruffy guy wearing pajama pants at the Redbox kiosk. I'd laugh my ass off.

Question: My daughter is invited to a sleepover where a PG-13 movie will be shown. My friend who is hosting the sleepover doesn't seem to think this is a problem, even though the kids are all just eight years old.

Ah, that feels so much better. The metaphorical stick up my ass (see above, if you're so rude as to read out of order) has been transported to you, rather like some sort of *Harry Potter* divination. I think a few of those were PG-13, too, and nobody much cared if you were eight as long as it was the boy-wizard movie. What's a little magical violence among friends? I've noticed that PG-13 movies can be wildly different. Sometimes it's as if the entire MPAA ratings team hasn't even watched the movie but just picks a rating, dartboard style, and immediately breaks for a long lunch of tequila shots. Find out what the movie is, watch it in advance, and make a decision based on your idea of what's right for your kid. Kidding! That's a whole lot of work. Just tell this lazy heifer that the kids are too young for that movie 'cause it's full of boobs and weed. That should do it.

Question: How do you handle it when a mom stays for a playdate? Our kids are seven years old, perfectly capable of playing together without us hovering. She seems to think I'm her playdate, but I have things to do. And, frankly, I don't like her that much. Why can't she just do a "dump 'n' run"?

It doesn't matter if you like her or not. You are using her kid to babysit your kid, and that's the way it should be. As a parent of an only child, I'll pimp my kid out all the time to play with someone else, just so I can have a moment to myself to work. Like right now. This woman is probably starved for adult conversation and is using her kid's visit as an excuse to hang out. While I understand that, I have little sympathy for such inconsideration. At the very, very least, she should ask if you have plans or if she can hang out. You are going to have to say something like: "I've got a ton of work to do, and so my plan is to ignore the kids until they scream or set something on fire." No? Okay. Greet them at the door, pull the kid in, and without letting her step inside, say, "You can pick up Jamie Sue at three o'clock. See you then!" Smile warmly and shut the door. If she protests (this is why you really have to shut the door), say in a cheerful tone: "I am so sorry, but I don't have time for a visit right now. We'll see you at three."

Question: *A couple of moms in our play group have said they have no intention of immunizing their children, because they believe this can lead to all sorts of problems. What do you think?*

I think your play group needs to not tell these moms where y'all are meeting next time. If they get pissy about it, just say that you've renamed your little group from Mothers' Morning Out to something more catchy, something like the Our Kids Don't Need Your Nineteenth-Century Deadly Diseases group.

If they act offended, tell them that while you respect their decision to subject their children to whooping cough, measles, and other long-dormant delights, you prefer to live in a safer, saner world where these diseases have very nearly been eradicated. Fuckin' weirdos.

chapter 12

Teen to Mom:
You're Not the Boss of Me
(Now Buy Me Something)

If you have a teenager living in your house, you may be vexed on a daily basis by what we in the South call "acting ugly." I'm not speaking of the Princess, of course, but your teenagers, who appear to be either sulky or high much of the time.

Okay, okay, maybe the Princess, at fifteen, isn't perfect, but I know how to handle it when she's not because I have channeled the ancient wisdom of my foremothers faced with the problem of a mouthy teen. If you take "our" advice, you, too, will have a much easier time when your teen is less than mannersome to you.

The time-honored secret? Embarrass the living shit out of your teen, and they will never, ever repeat the offending behavior.

A real-life example: The Princess was in a bad mood the other day as I drove her to theater dance class across town. She was uncharacteristically cranky (hormones, biology-test woes, they ran out of chicken tenders at lunch . . .) and was being quite rude to her mom-slash-chauffeur-slash-payer of her smartphone bill every month despite the fact that I only have a "stupid" phone my own self. Oh, how I give and give and give. But that's a story for another day. At this moment, the Princess was being quite testy and so I simply . . .

Rolled the windows down in my car, cranked up Kanye and Jay-Z's "Ni**as in Paris" and not only sang along at the top of my lungs but also began to chop the air with my arms in a most unbecoming middle-age white-lady dance move. I would not stop despite the Princess's increasingly hysterical pleas. Stopped for a red light at a very busy intersection, I "raised the roof" with my palms up, sending her sinking deep into the floorboard for fear of being seen.

By the time it got to the part where Kanye is bragging about his ability to acquire "bitches" at will, she was begging me to stop. She would behave. She would clean her room, even!

When you're talking teens, etiquette rules have to be a bit flexible. While I would normally find it unseemly to gleefully sing along to some really horribly misogynistic lyrics, the end justified the means. And to anyone unfortunate enough to have traveled on that stretch of roadway on that particular afternoon, I humbly apologize for my bad self.

Question: How can I convince my teenage son that manners matter? Whenever I mention cotillion classes, his eyes glaze over!

I believe we established that is because he is high. Okay, that's probably not true, but I think it's important for you to put yourself in your teen's place. Cotillion? Really? Today's teen doesn't want to be forced into an ill-fitting suit to dance with the girl in freshman class that he has honestly despised since kindergarten. Get creative with your approach. Tell him that if he continues to text at the dinner table, leave his sweaty soccer socks on the couch, and so on, there will be consequences. He will never listen until you take away his phone. Start there.

Question: I can't get my teenagers to write thank-you notes to their grandparents for birthday gifts. When they were little, I forced them to do it, but now that they're older, they never listen.

I can remember my grandmother sitting me and my sister down at her kitchen table and not letting us move from our chairs until we had dutifully written thank-you notes for birthday or Christmas gifts sent by her sisters. Even if Aunt Francis sent one dollar (which, allowing for inflation over the years—nah, who am I kidding—a dollar was still pretty much a crappy birthday gift even back in the day), we had to write heartfelt and flowery letters of thanks that were vastly (in my opinion) out of line with the gift itself. To wit . . .

What a delightful dilemma confronts me! How to spend this one dollar you have sent for my birthday? Will it be for a few Log Cabin or Chick-O-Stick candies? Or, perhaps the whimsical cellophane "fortune-teller fish" I've had my eye on each day I visit the Ben Franklin store after school with my best friend, Barbara Jean? Whatever I choose, please know that the dollar you sent me will afford endless hours of delight. I really can't say enough about your kind remembrance of my 10th year on Planet Earth. . . .

Yes, I actually wrote those words back in 19—— (sound of sputtering cough and whatnot). The point is, I understand how important it is to thank relatives, in particular. You won't look like an ungrateful little shit, and more important, you want to keep the gravy train rolling. My lengthy, butt-kissing thank-you notes resulted in gifts from these sweet old ladies for many, many years, and the amounts increased dramatically over time. Yes, it is true that one aunt accidentally gave me days-of-the-week crotchless panties for my high school graduation (I am *not* making that up), but other than that, I have found relatives giving gifts to be a wonderful thing.

Explain that the gifts will dry up soon because the grandparents have told you they're tired of your rude behavior. I don't care that you're lying about it; it could happen, and in the immortal words of George Costanza, "It's not a lie if you believe it's true."

Question: You mentioned texting at the dinner table. It's a huge problem for me. My teen insists on keeping her phone in her lap while we eat because, she says, "I could miss an important text." Despite my pleas, she always seems to sneak it into the kitchen. How can I convince her that it's incredibly rude to text at the table?

Oh, she knows it's rude; she just doesn't care. We have had the same problem with the Princess, who behaves as though every text is to confirm that a liver has just been made available and she must immediately depart to meet the transplant team. In reality, there is no such medical emergency (thank heavens!), only fluff about who's wearing what where and the like. It is maddening.

You have to be firm about this because studies have shown that families who eat dinner together at least four times a week really get on one another's nerves by that fourth night. No! I meant to say studies have shown the kids are healthier, happier, and make better grades than those who don't eat with their families at night.

It doesn't count if she's texting her friends while you're trying to be Perky Caring Mom, inquiring about everyone's day. Nobody gives much of a happy damn about your day, of course. If the texting continues ("Mom, you are so lame! What difference does it make?") you can smile a little drunkenly as you pass the tuna noodle casserole she actually likes and say, "If you don't put that phone in the other room during dinner, I will crush it, along with your spirit, beneath the wheels of the car you will never drive. Sweetheart."

Because you're just a little drunk, she will believe you. Trust me.

Question: How can I get my teenager to understand that it's very rude to act bored all the time. Also, he never looks adults in the eye, just stares down at his feet all the time.

Your kid sounds like pretty much of an asshole. I got nothin'.

Question: I'm a teenager who gets tired of my mom always asking, "Who are you texting now?" "What are you talking about?" "Who are you texting now?" "What are you talking about now?" She never stops asking intrusive questions when I'm texting my friends. Is it too much to expect her to show good manners and respect my privacy?

Oh, you poor, dear, sweet, misguided child. Of course it's too much to ask. She is your mother, the one who brought you into this world after what felt like eleventyhundred months of swollen ankles, hormonal back acne, and twenty-four-hour puking. But you go ahead and text your little friends. I'm sure that they would've sacrificed shellfish, soft cheeses, *and* vodka at the same time without a second thought just like I, I mean, your mother, did. One day, you'll miss hearing those nagging questions about what is most certainly your private and personal business. Little missy.

Question: My mom wears the same clothes I wear, and it's embarrassing. What can I do to get her to stop without hurting her feelings?

Clearly your mom did something right because you are interested in sparing her feelings, and that, my cherub, is the heart of good manners.

This is a sad trend, according to a study by the *Journal of Consumer Behavior*. Teenage girls are a huge fashion influence on what their mothers buy—not the other way around!

I was talking to the Princess about the study and realized that she was staring at me but not saying a word. Her eyes moved from head to toe. She took in my Toms shoes, jeans (not mom jeans—I'm not a damn Duggar, after all), and a T-shirt I bought at the Never Shout Never concert, which was totes cool, b-tee-dubs.

Said the Princess: "The study shows that we want our own identity, and then you copy us!"

"Yeah? Well, I want a million dollars. If you like the study so much, why don't you marry it?"

Part of the problem is a lack of choices for modern moms. Department stores are the worst for making us feel matronly what with their ghastly collections of plaid shirts layered over sad pedal pushers for the "mom on the go!" She must be going to rehab because she'd have to be crazy drunk or high to buy that shit.

What can I tell you except that you're right. And we'll try to do better. Cross my heart and hope to die (in Forever 21)!

Word to the wise: Teenagers don't always have a sense of humor. For instance, the Princess asked me to buy her student pictures with the "retouched package," which, for an extra fifteen dollars, removes blemishes, scars, flyaway hair; whitens dull teeth; and evens out skin tone. I said, "Sure, but you don't have flyaway hair," which seemed to piss her off.

Question: I am appalled at the language that I hear when I pick up my teenagers at school. Why must teens drop so many F-bombs? And what is wrong with them that they don't even seem to know you aren't supposed to curse like that in front of adults?

Yes, well, ahem, er, cursing. Right. Cursing is bad. No, strike that. Cursing is bad if done by young people in front of their elders. No, strike that, too. Okay. Young people should not curse, because, as everyone knows, cursing is a sign of limited intelligence. Someone read that to me from a book one time. Teenagers curse to sound grown-up, always have, always will. It's exacerbated because so many of the "cool people" they watch on TV curse constantly. Consider this made-up but totally possible convo from *Jersey Shore,* which is particularly popular with the teen demo. . . .

MIKE ("The Situation"):   Snooki is just a dumb (bleep) that I'd like to (bleep) on her (bleeping) (bleep) till she (bleeped), and then I'd be all like (bleeping) A!

SNOOKI: Mike's so stupid and he won't ever (bleep bleep) on you. I know that because his (bleeping) (bleep) of an ex-girlfriend (bleeping) told me that (bleep) and I (bleeping) believe that (bleep), (bleeping) A!

Now, it doesn't take a (bleeping) rocket scientist to figure out what each and every bleep means. It's like those word games people post on Facebook, where none of the words have vowels but you can easily read the whole thing anyway? The mind knows that shit. I mean stuff.

My advice? Give your best mean-face to the cussing teen. If that doesn't work, fuck it, you've done what you could to shame him.

Question: It's not as bad as cursing, but I find the new "vocal fry" very annoying. First it was using "like" every other word, then it was "uptalking," right? And now this weird guttural speech pattern. How can I correct this without being rude about it?

Ah, yes, vocal fry. To those who haven't been around teenage girls much, it refers to the odd lazy endings on words. Example: "interesting" becomes "interesteeeeeaaaaaaaaang."

I believe that, like toe socks and Clay Aiken, this will quickly become a thing of the past. Sorraaaaaaaay, Clay. Look, if drawing out a few syllables is the worst thing your teen does, count yourself lucky. He could end up on *Anderson Cooper,* talking about huffing glue and cinnamon or strangling himself to get high. By and large, today's teens aren't that much different from their parents at that age. Honestlaaaaaaaaaaay.

Question: My daughter, who will be sixteen soon, has been watching all those TV shows about rich people's kids having Sweet Sixteen parties, and now she expects a huge party and even a new car! How can I let her down easy?

By easy, do you mean a pan of brownies with a candle in the center and having a couple of girlfriends over for movie night? 'Cause that's what I plan. You know why? Because, unlike Timbaland, I can't afford that crap. I watched Timbaland's huge sixteenth bash for his son—whose name I forget, so I'll just call him "Splinter"—and it was nuts. I warned the Princess that she would *not* have a million-dollar bash featuring Lil Wayne, Missy Elliot, and live tigers.

"You don't want a party like those brats, do you?" I asked the Princess as we watched the daughter of the Ed Hardy T-shirt empire flicking her extensions about while auditioning male dancers for her soiree. Bubbles McVacant's dad gave her a pimped-out Land Rover for her sixteenth with her name written all over the outside of the car. Who does that? I mean besides Domino's.

Moments earlier, we'd watched Sean Combs's son present a ten-thousand-dollar check for Haitian relief at his party, which is swell until you realize that his party cost nearly a million and the check was just to make him look like slightly less of an asshat. Didn't work.

It should be noted that I don't begrudge the hardworking young. The Biebs bought himself a Lambo for his sixteenth. God knows he earned it, what with fending off marriage proposals from raspy-voiced twelve-year-olds every night. *Très* exhausting! Ditto Miley Cyrus, who worked hard for the money even as her nitwit dad was whining that *Hannah Montana* ruined his family. Oh, puleez. Disney doesn't kill families; families kill families.

As parents, we are charged with raising honest, capable, compassionate, well-mannered future leaders of America. These rich kids seem to have little knowledge of the world outside their own Rodeo Drive bubble. They're all "acting ugly." Pity.

chapter 13

Politics:

The Elephant (or Donkey)

in the Room

We know that it's impolite to talk politics, but sometimes we just can't help ourselves. So we dive in, with all good intentions of converting the ill-informed, the ignorant, and the outright idiotic, and, well, as you can see, things get nasty fast.

We just don't see things the same way. It's not our fault that you are so impossibly wrongheaded about all things political and we just can't understand why you bristle at our gentle corrections, which, yes, occasionally end with a "and your greasy *grandmama*!" followed by a slammed door.

Why do we all behave so rudely when talking politics these days? It's not just Rush Limbaugh, although his routine labeling of women who disagree with him as sluts, prostitutes, and "feminazis" certainly doesn't elevate the dialogue.

Politics is brutal business, not for the faint of heart and definitely an etiquette minefield.

We should all make an effort to have civilized discourse that relies on facts, logic, reason, and measured tones instead of name-calling, screaming, and finger-pointing.

Early on in the Obama presidency, I wondered if—and I'm being quite serious—he might not be a little too nice for the job.

If it had been me standing there, giving the 2009 State of the Union address when South Carolina congressman Joe Wilson screamed, "You lie!" I would've paused and quietly instructed the sergeant at arms to remove the old fart from the building, and possibly the planet.

Alas, he basically ignored this huge breach of congressional etiquette and continued as though nothing had happened.

Obama would make a lousy poker player. He'd be the pleasant sad sack who showed up every week in some buddy's heated garage, toting a six-pack of a nice pale ale and a decent amount of cash that he'd lose every time.

"Read 'em and weep," he'd say, fanning out a hand that boasted a one-eyed jack and not much else.

When trounced by assorted flushes, ace-high straights, and even two pair, he would remain evenhanded and calm.

"Just not my night, fellas," he'd say after going "all in" with a pair of deuces. Then, as they chuckled behind his back, he'd put on his black leather jacket and head into the cold night to live with his mother-in-law.

When Israel comes calling to ask if he'll drop everything and help them bomb Iran, Obama responds with an even tone and invokes the need for diplomatic rather than nuclear solutions.

He is Politenessman, which is laudable but frustrating to those of us who aren't quite so Zen about things.

I'm remembering that capitulation on unemployment benefits to the Republicans, who, as we all know, can't sleep at night if their billionaires are fairly taxed. Even Nancy Pelosi's cream cheese face melted into queso dip when Obama caved on that one.

He should've stood firm because I'm sure Boehner & Co. didn't have the Triscuits to return home at Christmas and tell their constituents they were cutting off their unemployment and Happy freakin' New Year!

These are challenging times. Can you imagine, even a few years ago, that you would see people holding signs saying THANK GOD FOR BREAST CANCER! as we did at Elizabeth Edwards's funeral? Being civil, returning deliberate, thoughtful responses to the crazy people is exhausting, isn't it?

I don't even know why someone would want to run for office. In a survey, fewer than half the people interviewed on the street knew the name of the vice president. And I'm not talking about an old dead vice president like the one who served under Zachary Taylor Swift. I'm talking about the one who lives at 1313 Mockingbird Lane, Washingtonville.

Not only did they not know his name, a scary number

thought that there were only fifty-two U.S. Senators and members of the House. Total. I suppose the thinking is one per state with a couple around as understudies in case somebody is too sick to perform that day or perhaps two Miss Congenialities.

It must be frustrating to spend $500 million to win an office only to discover that the average citizen doesn't know your name. You'd be better off changing it to Bob Evans, so at least people would say, "Love your stacked-and-stuffed hotcakes. Your Honorship."

Question: I think that so-called push polling is the height of rudeness, not only because of the nature of the questions but also because they call only at dinnertime.

I know, right? And I love the way they say, "This won't take long, maybe thirty or thirty-five minutes." Honey, you have *no* idea what I, and every mom I know, can get done in thirty-five minutes. It is staggering.

Push-polling is a dreadful—but dreadfully effective—political strategy. To those of you who don't know what it is, here's how it works. . . .

POLLSTER: Would you vote for Candidate A if you knew that he wanted to gamble with the financial security of your children and grandchildren?

YOU:	Huh?
POLLSTER:	It's true! And did you realize that Candidate A juggles dead puppies for his private amusement? Hmmmmm? He also wants to ship your job to China. Oh, and he wants you to pay twelve dollars a gallon for gas.

None of this is true, of course, but it sits in the back of your mind and marinates until you regurgitate it to someone else and they tell someone else and so forth until it morphs into "sorta fact." If you have the time, you can have some fun with push polls. For instance, if they go to the gas scare, say, "I'm so relieved to hear that. I've long thought that Americans shouldn't be paying roughly one-third as much as Europeans for gas. Don't you agree?" I've used this tactic more than once with pseudo-charities that call regularly.

PAID FUND-RAISER FOR RIP-OFF "CHARITY":	Wouldn't you agree we need better fire prevention education in our schools?
ME:	Heavens no! How else are our young American arsonists going to learn if not by experience?

See how easy?

Question: My friends ask me whom I'm going to vote for in every election. I think this is rude because I was raised to believe that voting is a private matter. Isn't that why they have those curtains around the voting machines, after all?

I guess so, but to me, those curtains are kinda weird. They look like really poorly designed dressing rooms. I've often thought it would be high-larious to close the curtain and then take off enough clothes to freak people out. When the bra hits the floor of the voting booth, that would be so funny, am I right?

I always leave the curtain open because I am proud of whom I vote for. This curtain business makes it seem like voting is something that should be done in the dark and is somehow secret and shameful, like attending an Adam Sandler movie.

But, of course, you are right. It's ill-mannered at best and nosy at worst to ask someone whom they're going to vote for. I'm happy to put up yard signs and even knock on doors for a good candidate (back in the '70s, this was rewarded with what we called "bong hits"), but not everyone is eager to share.

So, my advice would be to smile and say: "I don't like to discuss politics."

If they start yammering about why you should vote for

their candidate, you can say, *"I don't like to discuss politics."* Repeat as often as necessary.

Question: A neighbor who is running for reelection to local office is always in "campaign mode," no matter where she goes. I've even seen her show up at a funeral wearing her buttons and badges and (!) handing out magnets and bumper stickers. I'd like to set her straight but don't have the gumption.

Quick question: Is gumption grandpaspeak for "balls"? Thought so. While I do love a good refrigerator magnet because there's always some piece of kids' "artwork" I need to hang, having a candidate corner me in front of the corpse is fairly tacky. Local politicians can be surprisingly aggressive even when running for goofy offices like Soil & Water Conservation Supervisor. I've seen this sort of misbehavior in person, and it's off-putting at best.

Next time this happens, find your, uh, gumption and tell this opportunistic buffoon that "this is neither the time nor the place." Say it in a very imperious *Downton Abbey* kind of tone for greater effect.

Question: How can I convince my family not to talk politics when we get together for the holidays? My husband is the only non-Republican in the room, and he

*feels "ganged up on" most of the time. He's been a
pretty good sport so far, but he often wants to go home
before we even get to the pumpkin pie to avoid my father's bourbon-fueled soliloquy on how all liberals
are Communists. I honestly can't blame him.*

Holiday dinners are always minefields of misbehavior,
aren't they? It's the rare family, indeed, that can sit down, have
convivial conversation, and enjoy a nice meal without even a
whisper of tension.

The only thing you can do is to ask, in advance, that your
family shape the hell up and stop being so disrespectful of
your husband's opinions and beliefs. Really, it doesn't matter
what party anyone belongs to. Mutual respect and consideration are the point. Hot-button topics like politics have no
place at the holiday dinner unless you're sure everyone's on
the same page. If so, yes, have a side of sanctimony with that
corn bread dressing and green bean casserole, by all means.
If not, talk about the weather or how the only begotten grand-
son performed so beautifully in a small but telling role as
"third broccoli on the left" at his first-grade play.

I'm not saying it's going to be interesting, but at least your
husband won't feel the need to stab anyone with a meat fork
midmeal.

*Question: A friend of the family passed away, and her
obituary asked that mourners please, in lieu of flow-*

ers, make a contribution to the Republican party in her memory. I am having a hard time with this, as I am a Socialist. Can I just send flowers anyway?

I never cease to be horrified by these extraordinarily presumptuous requests nestled in the latter paragraphs of some obituaries. I've grown fairly much accustomed to the dreadful request for "donations to defray funeral costs" (shudder!) and to requests such as the one you have just mentioned. I always feel just a tad grief-stricken for all the florists out there who used to make a veritable killing off funeral flowers and now are reduced to making ends meet on prom corsages, Valentine's bouquets, and Administrative Professionals' Day, whatever the hell that is.

So, yes, by all means ignore the wishes of the family because they are, frankly, so unspeakably tacky, and send flowers or, better still, a nice peace lily that will live on until Uncle Snooky uses it to tamp out his cigarettes and it finally withers and dies.

Politics is personal. Don't hijack your loved one's funeral in this manner, even if she okayed it from her dotty old deathbed.

chapter 14

Always Leave Them Wanting More: The Art of the Visit

Visiting hours are over.

It's not just a phrase you hear around 9 P.M. if you're in a hospital. It's true of life in general. Growing up in the South, I was accustomed to the Sunday-afternoon drop-in. Everybody did it, usually visiting relatives that hadn't been seen since last Sunday and were most likely to have some homemade blueberry pie lying around somewhere.

No one would've thought of calling. It simply wasn't necessary.

Oh, how quaint it all sounds now. Also intrusive. But this was the way lives were updated, friendships were nurtured, and family ties were strengthened.

No more. Visiting hours are over. They have been replaced

with "Text me and maybe we can get together." If I sound a little peckish about the whole thing, it's because I am. I really miss that blueberry pie. I'd be lying if I didn't admit the system had its flaws. The true "drop in" always does. From the nosy in-laws dropping by on a Sunday afternoon just as you and your husband are, well, getting to know each other better, to the drop-in cousin who simply won't leave, because she has nothing else to do that afternoon. Who among us hasn't manufactured a "We were just on our way to . . ." when greeting an unexpected visitor? Better to tell a little tale than be held hostage in your home for upwards of three hours, am I right?

Still, I get a little misty-eyed when I think about lazy Sunday afternoons that brimmed with possibility. You never knew who might drop by or whom you might drop in on your own self. The Princess will never know of this grand tradition, and I find that a wee bit sad.

With visits, planned or unplanned, it's important to remember the number one rule of visiting etiquette: Always leave them wanting more.

Question: You mentioned the hospital visiting hours. I was recently in the hospital for a few days, and I was surprised how many people pay no attention whatsoever to visiting hours or how long they stay. I was exhausted, but visitors stayed and stayed in my room,

asking me questions and disturbing my rest. What's the correct etiquette on asking friends to leave you alone so you can recover?

Of course, it's cloddish to visit someone in the hospital and not pay attention to the telltale signs that it's time for you to go, such as heavy sighing by the patient, who is also pointing at an imaginary watch on his wrist. Some people are simply so caught up in the fabulous ambience of being in a tower filled with the sick and dying that they can hardly tear themselves away! Seriously, I say this only to remind you that, yes, visitors can be a pain, but it's no fun for them either. They're probably staying so long because it took them an hour to find a parking space, find someone who knows which room you're in, discover that you're no longer in that wing, find someone who knows your new room number, locate the right bank of elevators, remember that they forgot to bring you anything so then find the gift shop, buy flowers/card/balloon/stuffed animal/candy/book, et cetera, and then, finally, collapse in a tired heap in your one visitor's chair after a weary "How are you feeling?"

There are, you see, two sides to every story, as irritating as that is to realize. That said, you're absolutely within your rights to tell your visitor after, say, fifteen minutes that the nurse gave you something to help you sleep and you feel it "kicking in" right about now. As soon as they get out, you are welcome to crank up your pillow speaker and finish watching *Celebrity Wife Swap* until the next bedraggled visitor comes by. Damn! Doesn't anybody respect the ratings gold that is a Niecy Nash versus Tina Yothers smack-down on TV?

To the visitor: Please note that I said fifteen minutes. It's the perfect amount of time even if the patient appears to be enjoying your company immensely. You're probably not going to be the only visitor that day, or even that hour. Get gone.

Question: I love my in-laws, but they tend to drop in without calling. A lot. How can I ask them not to do this without sounding rude? I'm sure it will hurt their feelings.

Oh, yes. You're the ones doing the nasty on Sunday afternoons, right? And there, all set to harsh your mellow, are *his* parents, bearing gifts of homemade honey or some such and just wanting to watch the ball game with you. And could you rustle up something to eat, dear? They've driven nearly an hour, and they're famished!

Many advice columnists have dealt with this issue for many years, which is to say that this is not a new problem and it's not one that is going away anytime soon. In-laws can't be treated like a casual friend whom you don't have time to visit with (killing the lights and ducking below the windows when they knock on your door). No, no. This is family, and you have to tread lightly. Otherwise, you will become the least-favorite daughter-in-law, doomed to be introduced as "the one who doesn't really like us very much and we don't know why."

Your husband should be the fall guy on this one (and vice versa if it's her parents showing up unannounced). He should explain to his parents that they need to call ahead to make sure you aren't busy or have plans. They can't expect you to drop everything and entertain them after both of you have worked all week and managed, finally, to carve out some "couple time." But they will. Remind them, despite the wretched mental image this conjures, of what it was like when they were first married. Tact and diplomacy are called for here. Don't be a badass and don't be hostile. Be logical and kind.

It won't work, but you will have done the decent thing. Next time, draw the drapes and hit the floor.

Question: My husband's old college roommate drops by all the time, usually around dinnertime. He's single and unemployed. We have kids and our schedules are fairly rigid, but "college boy" doesn't seem to care. He just drops in, grabs a plate, and pulls up a chair. Have you ever?

No, I never. Okay, maybe once, but only once. Tell your husband to man up and tell "CB" that they're not in the dorm anymore, divvying up the weed and fighting over who's go-ing to camp out for Phish tickets. Look at it this way: You're enabling CB's bad behavior every time you let him intrude on your precious family time. He needs to find friends his own age, which, from the sound of it, is frozen at about twenty. These guys are as tenacious as the crabgrass that springs up on the front lawn of the darling house you're making mortgage payments on while this guy lives in a Pacer. You let them in your house more than once, and they'll never get out. Nip this in the bud. Yesterday.

Question: This is sticky. My neighbor loves to drop in because she knows that I work from home and I'm home all day. I like her a lot, but I can't seem to find the way to tell her that "work from home" means just that. I'd love to talk with her over a cup of coffee in my kitchen, but I can't do that and get my work done.

I work from home, so I can sympathize. Even though I've done this for more than fifteen years now after decades of working in an office, most of my friends really don't believe it's true. There have been times, many times, when I simply haven't answered the door. If I have a project with a deadline, I have to remember that these same people would never drop in on me in an office building for a coffee and chat session. It's really no different. So, although it sounds hostile and weird on the surface, I find that not answering the door (and the phone) gets the job done with no hurt feelings. If they say, "I dropped by, but I guess you were out for a walk," just smile and say, "I guess I was so caught up in finishing my work project, I didn't hear the doorbell." There is no need to say, "Yes! A walk! That's it!" or the transparently lame "I must've been in the shower."

Sometimes, you really do need a friendly break from work at home and the drop-in might be welcome. If so, enjoy, but remind yourself that, after an hour, it's time to go back to work. Let the drop-in know, too.

As with all things, this is much harder with relatives. Aunt Verlie, for instance, calls me two or three times a day. She always says, "You're not working, are you?" and I always say, "Yes, I am," and she always just blows right by that and continues her conversation. Caller ID is a wonderful thing. Use it.

Question: This isn't technically a visiting issue, but it sort of is. I wish my dad wouldn't "visit" my soccer games, because he always yells at the coach and embarrasses me. How can I convince him that he needs to stay home?

Your dad is the worst kind of visitor. The kind that shows up for a "visit" and then misbehaves in front of his family and his "host." With all the emphasis on kids' sports these days, I'm not surprised that this sort of thing is getting worse all the time. I know a ton of kids who spend every weekend being shuttled around the Southeastern United States for "traveling soccer," "traveling baseball," and even "traveling gymnastics," whatever the hell that is. The point is this: We've created a culture in which everything's a competition, and when that happens, people, including your dad, get a little crazy. Show him this section in the book, and tell him he's causing you emotional pain. Then tell him I said to stop acting like such an undisciplined asshat in front of his kid. I hate any situation in which the kid has to be the parent. Hate it.

chapter 15

Get a Clue in the Loo:

Restroom Etiquette

for the Lasses

I have a confession to make: One time, I used a men's restroom. It happened only once and it was an utterly horrifying experience. If it helps, you should know that I was with my friend Elizabeth at a Rolling Stones concert at Carter-Finley Stadium in Raleigh, North Carolina, and boy did we have to tee-tee.

Yes, grown women say that. It was a long walk from our wretched seats (Mick was just a faraway blur; he might as well have been SpongeBob, for all we could tell) to the ladies' bathrooms. When we got there, we quickly realized that a coup had been staged. Fed up with the ridiculous line, the women had taken over the men's restroom as well!

I'm not saying this was good manners; a coup often doesn't

concern itself with the social graces, after all, but I will say I understood, completely, the frustration at seeing *no* line in one huge restroom while the line to the ladies' room snaked around the complex all the way to the parking lot.

I don't want to repeat what I saw in that desperately dreadful place, except to say that it was far worse than anything I could've imagined. I have a vague memory of some sort of trough. There were only a few stalls with doors on them, as God intended, which we all made a dash for. As a distant Mick informed us that he would nevah, evah be our beast of burden, we did what we came to do, realized that, of course, the toilet wouldn't flush, and ran out of there like our clothes were on fire. Yes, yes, we washed our hands, but they felt dirtier afterwards, strangely.

All of this is by way of saying that I understand there might be different, very different, rules of etiquette for men and women using public restrooms.

For example, I cannot imagine a woman shouting to her neighbor in the next stall: "Lord, please! How 'bout a courtesy flush, sistah?" (For those of you with delicate sensibilities, a courtesy flush is an early flush of poo while one is still conducting one's business. It is used to mitigate the, ahem, odor. Please don't make me speak of this again.)

But I have been told by several men-type people that this notion is the height of good manners. Both the request for it and the resultant flush.

I know nothing of this culture of "courtesy flushes" because, of course, decent women never do their "serious business" in public toilets. Yes, yes, I suppose if you're caught unawares (stomach virus, dicey seafood gumbo, etc.) you could find yourself discovering, quite awfully and literally, that, yes, shit happens.

In general, however, this sort of behavior is to be avoided in public unless failure to address it would result in an even more horrendous violation of etiquette in polite company.

("Oh, heavenly days, Phillip, I do believe your date just beshat herself. Clearly she is NOKD." Not Our Kind, Dear.)

I have to confess to a sincere appreciation for scatological humor, so here's a story to ponder along those lines. . . .

A rather brash young British MP became overheated on the floor of Commons and mildly offended Winston Churchill. Party elders took the young man aside and said, "Look, we know that he's the opposition, but that is Sir Winston. You must visit his home and personally apologize for such a breach of etiquette."

Later that afternoon, the young man was driven to Chartwell, the Churchill estate, where he explained to the butler that he had to speak with Sir Winston on matter of great urgency. The butler excused himself and returned a few moments later to announce that Sir Winston was currently indisposed. The young MP grew even more anxious and said, "I *must* speak with him and I am willing to wait." The butler disappeared again and returned several minutes later to say: "Sir Winston says for me to relay that he can take only one shit at a time."

I just love historical bathroom humor, don't you? And speaking of things historic . . .

Question: This is a delicate subject but I need guidance. My son's fiancée knows that we have old plumbing in our historic home, yet she continues to flush her female, uh, accessories, down the toilet whenever she visits. This always necessitates a visit from the plumber the next day and a subsequent two-hundred-dollar bill at the minimum. How can we ask her to stop doing this? Should I present her with the plumber's bill?

Oh, dear. She's flushing Coach purses and Vera Wang scarves down your toilet? What an odd girl.

Kidding! I know that you're talking about tampons, but really, "accessories"? You get style points for quaint. We do not walk about with tampons dangling from our earlobes, for heaven's sake. Well, maybe Barbara Walters, but really, no one else comes to mind.

That said, you have asked a delicate question in a caring way, and so I will respond in like manner.

What the hell is wrong with you? Surely she knows that this is unacceptable, because I'm sure your idiot son has told her. What's that? He's too shy to mention it?

Wait a minute. Aren't these two engaged? Which means they're regularly bumpin' uglies? And he's too shy to tell her to quit tearing up your family throne every time she visits?

Admittedly, I am more sensitive to this issue than most, as I live in a ninety-year-old house with plumbing that requires neonatal-intensive-care levels of tenderness. In fact, if anyone asks to use our bathroom, I give them a good five-minute lecture on what is acceptable and what is not. Sometimes, it's so off-putting that the guest, utterly defeated, decides to go home instead. Which is fine because, really, how many times do you have to hear: "You know what they say? You don't buy beer; you just rent it!"

Tell her that she's ruining your plumbing with her indiscriminate flushing of unmentionables. If she does it again, yes, by all means, present her with the plumbing bill. She sounds like a colossal dumb-ass; it may take a visual to get this one to shape up. Speaking of visuals, you could install a lovely framed and severely calligraphied warning just above the toilet:

Please refrain from flushing personal products;
our elderly plumbing can't take it!
Thank you.

Question: The other day I recognized the shoes of a coworker in the next stall. She left before I did, but I

never heard her wash her hands. Since she frequently brings and serves treats to us in the break room, should I say something?

Oh, no. It would be much better to grab a couple of those butterscotch brownies and dig in, relishing the extra flavor zing from the *E. coli* coursing through your system with each bite. Jesus, did you see the movie *Contagion?* I did. And let me just say that now I know that the entire planet is just one misplaced bat turd falling into a suckling pig in Mongolia away from complete annihilation.

Of course you should call her out, publicly if possible, and definitely before anyone has the chance to dive into Germapolooza. Tell her that you know that she doesn't wash her hands after she pees (and probably the other), and that's just gross. It's a brave move, granted, and it's definitely a friendship buster. But you don't need to hang out with such an inconsiderate cow anyway.

Question: Why do so many women hover over the toilet, leaving pee spray on the seat when there are perfectly good seat protectors in a wall dispenser that could be used and then flushed away?

While I always believe one should wipe away one's "pee spray," as you so colorfully call it, I'm afraid I'm less than reliable when it comes to using those disposable paper seat protectors because I don't like getting too intimately involved with the process. What process? you ask. That's easy. . . .

Pull out seat protector.

Watch it disintegrate in your hands.

Pull out second seat protector and try to punch out poorly perforated center section.

Affix seat protector to seat without using your hands. (This one is particularly challenging.)

"Aim" your pee through the punched-out hole in the seat protector.

Realize too late that you've completely missed the open hole in the center, and the pee is now trying to physically find its way back into your body.

Give up, stand up, and accept that the thing isn't going to be sucked down into the bowl by the act of flushing, the way it's designed to do.

Kick the flimsy and wet paper into the toilet bowl with your foot.

Now do you get it? It's just a lot of work. I'd rather hover, although my knees are getting increasingly arthritic, since you ask, and I may just bag the whole thing and plop down on the seat, risking STDs and unwanted pregnancy and God knows what-all else. Next?

Question: What do you do if you're a man who is urinating in a public restroom and another man seems to be staring at your private parts?

I dunno, Chaz. Maybe they're just confused as hell.

I'm told that it's common courtesy to leave a buffer of at least one urinal between you and whomever. It's creepy not to and really no different from the guy who sits right beside you in a near-empty movie theater. Nuff said.

TP (Tips to Ponder!)

- If you're in an airport, or a nice place, you may encounter a bathroom valet with a tip jar and a depressingly pedestrian assortment of off-brand mints, mouthwashes, lotions, and the like. Just give him or her a dollar and get on with your life. If you ever need eight-year-old floss, she or he will be there for you.

- Gentlemen, do not tap your toes in a stall. I have it on good authority that such behavior could turn you into a Republican congressman.

- Don't take too long. This means don't use a public restroom to read your Kindle. (Unless, of course, it's this book, in which case, well, Godspeed!) Don't sit there and do puzzles or send e-mail, and for the love of all that is holy, do *not* conduct cell phone calls for either business or pleasure while seated on the toilet. I've heard women do this and then flush, so they don't even *care* that the person on the other end of the line knows that they're talking while peeing. Horrible!

- If you are using the restroom at a friend's house, leave the seat down. Just do it. It looks prettier, and my germ-phobic friend, Amy, swears that you should always make sure to flush with the seat down so "cooties don't fly all over the room." Makes total sense.

- Admittedly, this isn't so much an etiquette issue as a commonsense one: Should the toilet paper face front on the roll, or should it curl behind? Both have pluses and minuses, but it just looks better facing out. I have a childlike delight in the clever things hotel maids can do to gussy up a simple end flap of toilet paper, none of which could be accomplished with the paper on the inside, against the germ-ridden wall. (Okay, that was Amy again.)

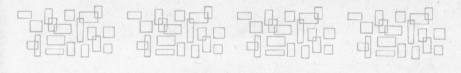

chapter 16

"Your Toupee Looks So Natural!"
How to Give and Receive
Compliments

Has anyone ever told you, "You really need to learn how to take a compliment"?

Because, believe it or not, there's a right way and a wrong way to give—and receive—compliments.

I know what you're thinking: "Isn't it enough that I said something nice? Why you gotta analyze everything?"

Okay, first of all, "why you gotta?" and second of all—oh, just forget it.

We're also going to talk about "left-handed compliments," which, as a proud lefty, I find a tad offensive. Just a tad. I am now over myself and have already moved on.

How to Take a Compliment

This is particularly difficult for those of us who were raised in the South, where we'd rather plunge a butter knife into our own larynx than utter a single unpleasant word—to your face, that is.

We consider it unseemly to agree with any kind words thrown our way. Yeah, I know it's weird, but we are trained to repel compliments as though shielded by a protective force field that will simply take the compliment ("Your hair looks lovely today") and reflect it immediately back upon the giver ("No! I'm having a horrible hair day. But yours looks ah-mazing!"). This boomerang effect leaves the giver of the compliment wondering why she or he even bothered.

For shit's sake, just say thank you. And if it's true and you feel that you must, you can add, "Yours looks nice, too." Was that really so hard?

There's nothing wrong with receiving a compliment with a simple and gracious, "Thank you!" In fact, it's preferred. In the South, we are trained not to brag or put ourselves before others (which is why it's such a shock when we hear others do it, as we discuss in another chapter).

It can be vexing for a non-Southerner to have the last word when it comes to giving a compliment. Here's an example of how difficult it can be.

NS: That's a beautiful scarf. And the color is so perfect on you!

S: Oh, it's all right, I suppose. I think the color would look even better on *you*!

NS: Nonsense, it matches your eyes perfectly.

S: Here, you take it. I think it would look best on you. I've always envied your skin tone. My skin is as green as a toad under most artificial lighting, but yours? You're positively glowing!

NS: Thank you. Let's change the subject. Hey, wait. What are you doing? Are you taking the scarf *off*?

S: You bet I am. I want you to have it. Really. It will look so much better on you than me. . . .

NS: Okay, you're right. You're an ugly old hag with a gray face and yellow teeth, and I'll look much better in the scarf than you!

S: I know you're joking, but really, I've been thinking about getting Lumineers. How did you know?

NS: I give up. Give me the damn scarf. I'm outta here.

The Left-handed Compliment

Oh, you know the ones I'm talking about. Perhaps you've even delivered one and then walked away, rather enjoying its effect on the recipient. Or you could say it and not mean any harm at all. You just don't think before you speak; work on that.

While the most outlandish example imaginable was the title of my last book, *You Don't Sweat Much for a Fat Girl,* most people would never actually say such a thing. I hope. Need more examples? Okay. Never say things like . . .

- Wow! You drive well for a woman.
- This casserole tastes almost as good as the one Mama makes.
- That dress sure does wonders for your body type.
- Your new toupee almost looks real!
- I don't care what everybody says, I think you're a nice person.
- President Obama is very articulate.
- I like your hair; it makes your head look smaller.
- You have great birthing hips.

Question: Well, all of that is fine and good, but what about people who never give compliments, left-handed or otherwise? My sister has never given me a compliment in my life, in spite of the fact that I've always been supportive and caring toward her.

Your sister is insecure and a bit jealous, I suspect. She is under the wrongheaded impression that if she compliments your work, clothing, hairstyle, cooking, home, garden, and so forth, this actually makes her seem inferior. Nothing could be further from the truth. It's the mark of a generous, openhearted person to give compliments lavishly and sincerely. If only she understood that. You sound lovely, by the way.

Question: You know, it would be really nice to just once have a man compliment my archery or volleyball skills or even my elegant penmanship. Instead, I get "Nice rack!" or something equally juvenile. Why do men have to be so superficial?

Hmmmm? What? Oh, I'm sorry, your rack was distracting me with its awesomeness. I don't want to call you a liar, but I can't imagine anyone saying, "Nice rack!" to your face (or to the rack in question). If you walked by a group of drunks at a sports bar and one of them said it, that's different. Some men are dunderheads when they drink, so there's no telling what you're going to hear in the way of a "compliment." All men aren't superficial, just as all women aren't uptight bitches with really nice handwriting. Just saying.

Question: I'd love to be complimented on the work I do, but my boss manages to hog all the glory, taking credit for other people's good ideas, including mine. I know he knows better. Should I confront him about this?

That depends. He could fire you or make your life difficult if you speak up. In the interest of keeping a job you genuinely like and at which you excel, I would settle for the occasional

"We all worked on this as a team!" whenever it seems appropriate in front of higher-ups. It should seem natural, not forced, and you can monkey around with the wording to suit the occasion. The object is to call out your jerk of a boss without seeming to make it personal.

Question: I know that it's important for kids to have positive reinforcement so they will have a good self-image, but isn't there such a thing as being too complimentary? My friend compliments her young children constantly. I maintain that it's too much of a good thing. Do you agree?

Yes. We've all seen and heard those ridiculous playground moms who heap praise on their children for completing the simplest task.

"Oh, Frankie! I can't believe how you spent the whole day breathing in and out! Way to go, sweetie!"

This sort of foolishness will, trust me, result in Frankie becoming the biggest turd at Positive Reinforcement Preschool and Child Development Academy. When the teacher corrects him, he'll melt down and wonder if it's possible that he's not all that special after all. It's not only possible; it's likely.

Children should be complimented and praised for genuine accomplishments. If you start gushing every time your kid remembers to flush his pee, he's going to expect a ticker tape parade for doody. It will never end. Next thing you know, he'll want high fives and hot doughnuts for simply managing to walk down the sidewalk without busting his ass every day. Enough!

Question: I've recently lost a great deal of weight . . . 145 pounds, to be exact. I'm proud of my accomplishment and I do like it when people say how nice I look, but it makes me wonder if they thought I was hideous before. When I think about it that way, I can't enjoy the compliment at all.

Congrats on the weight loss. Now you need to gain some perspective, which, fortunately, weighs almost nothing. It would be odd indeed if your friends, family, acquaintances, and most especially people who haven't seen you for a while, didn't acknowledge your weight loss with a well-earned compliment. I know a woman who went from 306 (at five foot two) to 140 pounds after two solid years of counting Weight Watcher points and exercising. It would've been bizarre if I didn't tell her how wonderful she looked the first time I saw her after the weight loss.

Does this mean that she didn't look good before the weight loss? Frankly, yes. She wasn't "hideous," but she looked miserable and unhealthy. It's not about pretty versus ugly. It's about slowly becoming healthy and strong. You've worked incredibly hard to give yourself an amazing gift here. The trick now is to reconcile your new look with your old insecurities. You can do this.

Question: Wow. That sounded really sensitive and smart. You're not so bad at this advice-giving thing.

I know, right? I mean, "Thank you."

chapter 17

*

Road Sage:
Accept the Things You Cannot Change,
Like Idiot Drivers

The driver in front of me had inexplicably left at least three car lengths between his car and the one ahead of him. WTF?

Okay, here's something the Emily Vandersnoots and so forth never wrote about in *their* etiquette books: Most drivers are basically inconsiderate assholes. And that includes you and sometimes me.

But usually it's you.

So here's the scenario: The light has turned green at this hugely busy intersection in my hometown, and Slowpoke McDumbass is driving very sloooowwwly toward the intersection. Remember, he's still got three car lengths to catch up. I'm right behind him, and guess what? That's right! He cruises sloooowly through the intersection just as the light turns red.

So here I sit, pissed beyond all rational behavior, as I watch him totter on in the distance, leaving me to sit at the head of the line waiting for another 2.5-minute cycle to pass.

I want to disembowel him. (Using the correct cutlery, of course.)

I hear you: "What's your hurry?" or "Life's too short to sweat this small stuff!" or "Why, yes, as a matter of fact, I *have* had a lobotomy."

Normal people don't drive that way. I realize that some of us have personal-space issues (more on that in another chapter), but the highway is no place to work through them.

Do not leave three car lengths; hell, don't even leave one! Proper driving etiquette demands that you basically get close enough to the car in front of you at a busy intersection that it would mean that in certain third-world countries, or South Carolina, you would have to get married.

One of the things that irritate drivers who are new to life in the American South is that we natives don't use turn signals. This is not only bad driving etiquette; it's also unsafe. What can I say? I've spent a lifetime explaining that we don't use turn signals because we know where we're going and it's nobody else's damn business.

But I know it's rude, and I'm gonna stop. It's just that, like making the transition to turkey bacon, it hasn't been easy. (I'm just kidding, of course; that shit tastes awful.)

So, my own sin confessed, let's return to yours: Drivers who don't use the turning lane. I can't tell you how many times I've witnessed this violation of driving etiquette. Once, I witnessed a frustrated driver flip off another driver who turned left from the "motorway," as the slutty-sounding British chick inside my GPS likes to call it, without using the turning lane.

Question: When confronted with rude drivers such as you have just so cleverly described, is it ever okay to indicate annoyance and displeasure through the use of obscene hand gestures?

No. Let me put it another way. . . . Hell no. This is because, as Aunt Verlie reminds me almost daily: "He could have a gun under his car seat and he could reach down there and get it and blow your brains out all over your leather-look vinyl seats."

In the South, because we are all, frankly, packin', this is not an entirely baseless fear, this notion that road rage will result in death or, at the very least, a good old-fashioned case of what Verlie likes to call "your basic permanent disfigurement."

It goes without saying that you should never do what my

friend Sam did when a rude driver pulled out in front of him, forcing him onto the shoulder to avoid a collision. Sam, catching the other driver's eye, simply mouthed the word "Douchebag!" and, well, it was on like unto *Donkey Kong.*

DB responded by mouthing the word "Cocksucker!" and the two of them drove along like this, side by side, for at least a couple of miles, finally exhausting their somewhat limited vocabularies.

Ultimately, Sam had to resort to "Turtlehead!" which lacked the impact of his earlier expressions and left the other driver mouthing, "What? What did you just call me?" At this point, it really was over. And high time.

Teach Your Children Well

It's hard to believe, but we're already teaching the Princess how to drive. As we hovered over her crib fourteen years ago, watching her sleep and listening to the stuffed bear that made *whoosh-whoosh* womb sounds (kinda gross, now that I think about it), Duh Hubby and I never gave a thought to driver's education.

But here we are. My kid will be a well-mannered driver if it kills us. I have to admit, so far, she's almost obnoxiously cautious, placing her hands on the wheel and muttering "ten and two," adjusting the seat, all the mirrors and—*for God's sake are we ever going to go somewhere?* Sorry. That was me. The truth is, I have been relieved of my coaching duties, owing to some tearful accusations that I told her to run over a squirrel.

Which I did, but it's not as bad as it sounds.

"Always remember," I said, buckling in for safety, "if something jumps in front of you, run over it. You have no idea how many people die every year, trying to avoid hitting a squirrel or something. You are more important than a squirrel."

I know! That kind of parental wisdom just oozes out of me like cheese out of an Egg McMuffin.

I didn't tell her about the time I was so sleep-deprived as a new mommy that I strapped her to my chest in a BabyBjörn and drove all over town doing errands with her attached to my front like a really well-dressed little air bag.

I did, however, tell the Princess that a recent study found that children watch how you drive, and if you're steering with your knees while you add cream to your coffee, texting and curling your eyelashes, they'll do the exact same thing.

Which means I'm off coffee for a while. Also eyelashes.

After an hour or so of driving around a church parking lot without incident, I took back the wheel and drove us home, feeling happy and sad at the same time. Happy because the Princess seemed to be a cautious, etiquette-conscious driver in the making. Sad because I forgot to TiVo *Breaking Bad* the night before. What? You were expecting something more introspective?

Okay, how about this? Did you know that in Saudi Arabia, women aren't allowed to drive? I'm not sure who does the carpool every day at Riyadh Preschool Learning Environment ("Where Every Kid Is Terrific!") or who picks up the burka at the $2.25 Cleaners or who takes little Abdul to the orthodontist for the eighty gazillionth check on his spacers. Not to mention who takes *his* mother for her podiatry appointment twice a year.

The reason given for not letting Saudi women drive is that the male leaders believe it will lead to premarital and extramarital sex. What the hell is on that driver's test? It must be a lot more challenging than parallel parking.

I told the Princess that she was lucky to live in a country like the USA, where she can't be jailed for simply "driving while female." Rage on, Saudi sisters. We have your back.

Parking Lot Do's and Don'ts

Oh, where to start? Oh, I know! With a true story . . .

Last week, we had twenty-four inches of rainfall in two days in my hometown. I needed groceries because we were down to having toothpaste for supper, so out I went, into the storm, with the dedication of a pioneer woman forced to forage for high-quality frozen lasagna for her family.

There were lots of fools like me out in the rain, but I chose my store carefully because it has a marvelous overhang thingy that helps you stay out of the rain while loading your groceries at the curb.

I left my filled cart at the curb in the clever groove that keeps it from rolling into the parking lot, presumably in search of a happier life. But when I drove up, I discovered a van parked smack in the middle of the loading area. A woman sat in the van, unaware that her Very Own Private Parking Spot, uh, wasn't.

I tapped gently on my horn. Notice I said "gently." I hate it when people honk like you're getting ready to run over a toddler. Even if you're getting ready to run over a toddler. So, yes, I tapped gently—almost Zen-like, if you can imagine that.

No response.

More gentle tapping, and, well, finally I had to approach her window, where I wanted to shout: "Move your car, you mouth-breathing malingerer" but instead said, "Please move up; I'm going to get soaked."

She grunted, polished off her Funyuns, crumpled the bag, tossed it into the back of her odious van, and moved up. Just a little. Bitch.

I still got fairly much soaked. I looked, with sympathy, at the line of cars forming behind me, then made huge circles in the air beside my temple and pointed at the van. The man in line behind me smiled softly. What had he been smoking?

The moral: Think of others, all the time. Not Funyuns. Others. See? Not so hard, is it?

Driving etiquette may be even more important in parking lots. How many times have we staked out a spot in a crowded lot, turned the blinker on to signal our intentions, waited for the car to back up, and watched another car whip in ahead of you and claim your space.

She didn't even signal!

In this circumstance, and only this one, you have only one possible response, and that is to key the offender's car. Discreetly, of course. You don't want to end up in one of those ghastly mug shot magazines with your startled face and bad hair right beside the child molesters, Lohans, and those wacky Amish beard-cutters. When you do key the car, be sure to bear down and go super deep so they can't just get the half-price fix at Maaco. Not that I would know anything about any of that.

Summary Because You Know You Won't Remember All This Stuff

- Tailgate at all intersections.
- Use turn signals and turning lanes unless you don't wanna.

- Squirrels suck.
- Refrain from cursing at or gesturing at other drivers, no matter how much they deserve both, because they could kill you and, thus, make you super late for work.

chapter 18

Foreign Affairs:
Stop Making Me Feel Stupid with
Your Fancy Multilingualism

One of the vilest breaches of etiquette is to speak to others in a foreign language while in the company of people who speak only English. Yeah, I said it.

Please save your righteous indignation. I don't want to hear that if we were European, where even the average dumb-ass (Russell Brand) can speak four or five languages, this would be less of a problem, so of *course* it's our fault for being so hopelessly bourgeois to begin with.

While some of you might consider this brutally unenlightened, I'm afraid that this would come under the category of a "you" problem.

I'm not asking for fluent English at the Korean nail salon, for instance. I'm just asking for good manners. In other words, why must you scrutinize my pitifully rough heels and then scream very loudly to your coworker something that sounds like *"Dong chow hok wad ho!"*

It only makes it worse when the coworker scurries over, glances down, and laughs out loud. I mean doubles the hell over, she's laughing so hard. Not cool.

Ah, laughter. The universal language. So I laugh, too. And then they abruptly stop. For a horrible second, they might think that the one yokel in Eastern North Carolina who speaks Korean has landed in their mall spa, and ain't they got all the luck?

I can only imagine that *"Dong chow hok wad ho!"* is Korean for "Oooh, birthday pedicure. Big spender! She gets her toes painted once a year whether they need it or not!"

One time, after one of these foreign exchanges with her coworker, the technician giving me the pedicure returned to look at me with something approaching genuine sorrow:

"You work in garden *all* the time, miss?"

See? She might not speak English, but she can speak fluent bitch, am I right?

I truly love these nail places because they're fast, reasonable, and there's a better-than-average chance that one of the pictures on the wall will have one of those moving waterfalls in it. I love that shit. And I love how, if they're busy, they just text more techs, who magically appear in under a minute. Are they beamed in from the pretzel kiosk? How is that even possible?

As an aside, there is one very odd aspect to a visit to my mall nail spa: The TV is always on. It's a huge flat-screen, mercifully closed-captioned, because it's always playing the same DVD of a young samurai slaying a village, and really, it's a tad violent to see while you're getting your calves massaged with eucalyptus oils.

Wordless bloodletting overhead aside, customer service wise, we're all good. It's just the language thing that needs to change.

I realize that there are a few English phrases that are memorized, but what amazes me is that there must be a list of "possible responses from the bossy American" who happens to be at your station.

"New glitter acrylic?" a technician who can speak almost no English inquires.

"No thank you," I respond.

She assumes a big, oversized look of sorrow, as if I just strangled her kittens. Trust me, there is really nothing sadder than the face of a Korean nail tech who experiences the firm decline of a service upgrade.

She looks so sad that I hastily explain that I'm a little "long in the tooth" for that sort of stuff.

The idiom only confuses her further, and we are off to a very rocky start. I'm afraid she might apply yin–yang symbols to my teeth, at this rate. I decide that if she does, I won't complain. And overhead, the young samurai has just disemboweled another villager at the exact moment I'm offered "soothing sugar scrub no charge?"

"Uh, no thanks. I like my disembowelments with an eyebrow wax usually."

She looks confused, and I realize that I have been kind of a shit, so I say, "Sorry. Yes. Sugar scrub, please."

I don't want to be the Ugly American. Inside or outside.

Question: My daughter-in-law is from another country, and when we all get together for holidays, she and her family never speak English, which leaves me feeling left out and foolish. I feel like they are talking about me. What can I do?

Well, I hope you've been paying attention because, yes, of course they're talking about you. Was it the part where they pointed at you and giggled behind their hands that gave it away? Wow. You truly *are* the sharpest tool in the shed, aren't you?

Rude is rude in any language, so the only thing you can do is to say something like: "Please speak English. I can't understand you." This will be much more effective if you yell it at the top of your lungs.

Kidding! Don't yell, but do make it very clear that you're completely pissed off. I mean, really, who do they think they are? You gave them your *son,* after all, and while he was a classic underachiever and, if we're being honest, you never loved him quite as much as his younger brother, he's very much in love with a woman who, despite her own flawless English, purposely leaves you out of the conversation whenever her parents are around.

Although I generally detest "walking a mile in someone else's shoes" or "trying to look at an issue from both sides," this really may be the exception.

After all, how frustrating it must be for them to hear you prattle on in English about your great-aunt's buttermilk pie recipe as you serve it. They don't have a freaking clue, so stop trying. Just slice the pie, shove the plate at them, and go back to your bedroom and watch *The King of Queens*.

Do not emerge from your bedroom until your son has taken his wife and "those people" aside and explained that you're feeling left out, and while it's true that you can be an overwrought, demanding handful even if everybody in the room is speaking perfect English, they really are being fundamentally ill-mannered.

You'll want to hear all of this, so while I don't generally condone eavesdropping (well, actually, it's my third favorite pastime after scrapbooking and drinking too much), remember it really does help to keep your ear pressed to a juice glass at the door to listen in. You won't want to miss a word! Except perhaps that part about being overwrought and demanding.

Question: Why can't we look at this differently? Being a monolingual society isn't anything to brag about, now, is it?

America is hardly monolingual. For instance, as a Southerner, I speak fluent redneck, so this makes me somewhat bilingual. I usually try to have a "when in Rome" philosophy when it comes to deciding which "language" to use. I meant Rome, Georgia, of course. This isn't language hypocrisy; it's just about knowing who you are and where you are. If you're not skilled at this, you can end up the butt of the joke.

My friend's cousin moved up north and returned home for a visit after a couple of years. The family had a good laugh at her expense after days of listening to her talk "citified" when she let slip, during a tour of the farm, "Oh, my, the 'baccy is certainly growing tall this year."

While I don't generally condone "putting on airs" or "getting above your raisin'," there are times when we instinctively know to drop the redneckspeak. If, for instance, someone who looks anything at all like Pierce Brosnan walks into the room and he's interviewing you for your dream job, it's time to retrieve your dropped g's, stop announcin' what you're "fixin' to do," and resume being the clever worldly woman you are. We know how to talk proper; we choose not to.

And now a question, directed at me, from my good friend Shelley: You know that thing you do every single

time we go out to dinner and you've had a couple of beers and you tell me to "Talk German! Y'all listen. Really. She sounds so cool. Go ahead!" Well, I just hate that. I'm not a show dog, for heaven's sake.

Well, ouchenstein, Shelley. I had *no* idea you felt this way, and I am so very sorry. Really, really sorry. I mean, the last thing I would want to do is piss off a German. Just sayin'.

Shelley says, correctly, that asking her to "talk German" shouldn't be a party game, and it's just as demeaning as pointing a gun at someone's feet and telling them to "Dance!"

I know that she's right. I hate it when someone recognizes me and says: "Hey! Say something funny!" Which I never can. I can't even tell a decent dirty joke, much less be funny on command. Inevitably, I apologize for being so lame and they walk off mumbling to one another stuff like, "Damn, I thought she'd be funnier." Yeah, well, I thought I'd be smarter, richer, and thinner, too, but shit happens. Deal with it.

Politeness: The Universal Language

- No matter how much you want to, never invite someone who is speaking a foreign language in your presence to "Go back to your country." The only time that phrase is ever acceptable is if you are British and you are speaking to Madonna. In this case, I believe I speak for Queen Elizabeth, Charles, William, Kate, and even Kate's sister (the pretty little thing who had to wear a fake ass to the royal wedding) when I say "Godspeed."

- If you are speaking English in the ladies' room at the Ramada because you are at your cousin's *quinceañera* and I walk in because, while I don't know your cousin, I really need to pee and then you, like, look at each other and then immediately start speaking in Spanish, well, amigas, it is *on*. Because I have three years of high school Spanish under Mrs. Vega, and she was *muy* tough. See, I can understand what you bitches are saying. Although it is something of a mystery why you think "the maroon llama likes the chicken to go to the library."

chapter 19

Facebook Etiquette:
An Oxymoron

Facebook is fertile ground for etiquette violations.... The lover who learns she's been jilted when her boyfriend suddenly changes his relationship status to "single"...the pesky, impersonal pleas to participate in time-sucking games and quizzes and calendars and causes...the endless (and mostly mindless) political rants...the unauthorized use of that photo of you sucking the remains of a Jell-O shot from some cabana boy's navel in Key West.

But really. Need I go on?

True story: Just this morning a Facebook "friend" posted a ghastly photo of a dead dog on my home page while urging me to join her pet-adoption cause.

Unfriend. Unfriend. Unfriend.

Question: I really want to unfriend someone because she puts so many obnoxious posts on Facebook. We're

not real-life friends, just went to high school together, but it could be awkward at the upcoming reunion if she knows I defriended her.

Well, which is it? Defriend or unfriend? Don't get me wrong; I don't really care; I'm just asking. Either way, this is what you get for accepting friend requests from former classmates because you naïvely believe that you'll somehow like this person way more than you did twenty-five years ago, when you caught her blowing your boyfriend under the bleachers at the homecoming game. And remember how it stung when she just shrugged those little toad shoulders of hers and said, "Well, somebody had to do it," like he was going off to war and all he wanted was this big ol' blow job before he left?

Even if it wasn't something that "grody," as you used to say, the fact is, you weren't real-life friends then, and you shouldn't be Facebook friends now. Who really cares if she acts huffy with you at the reunion? You don't need her or her tired-ass status updates ("I'm making pudding tonight!") to punctuate your day, do you?

And speaking of status updates, the worst ones have some app or the other that tells your friends where you are at that very moment. (By the by, it took me quite a while to realize that "app" is short for "application" not "appetizer," and now that I know that, I don't care at all anymore.) I have a FB friend whom I truly love in real life, but she simply must stop these updates of "Manda Sue is at Best Buy," followed thirty minutes later by "Manda Sue is at Olive Garden." It's not as if when I see her later this week, I'm going to say, "Oh my gosh! I saw where first you were at Best Buy and then you were at Olive Garden and then . . ."

You know why? Because *I don't give a fuck.* So, yes, unfriend this "friend" and move on. Proper etiquette dictates that you should never deliberately hurt someone's feelings, but proper etiquette also dictates that you shouldn't blow someone else's boyfriend. I remember Emily Post writing something about that one time. . . .

Question: I keep getting invitations to "events" that take place up to three thousand miles away. It seems rude not to respond, but really, there's very little chance that I will fly fifteen hundred miles to see my ex-boyfriend's Lynyrd Skynyrd tribute band perform at a bar in Cootertail, Texas, am I right?

Well, I don't know. Are they really good? Or do they just do one half-assed Skynyrd cover after another? I'd pretty much crawl nekkid over a field of broken glass to hear a decent cover of "Free Bird." Okay, I'm getting sidetracked here. Let's pretend you asked about going to an Average White Band tribute band performance instead. Yeah, that'll never happen.

As with so much of what passes for an "invitation" in these days of social media, the truly etiquette conscious may wonder how to properly reply. The answer is simple: You respond in kind. If someone, for instance, tweets their wedding shower invitation, you are within your rights to tweet back, in 140 characters, that despite the obvious love and care they have demonstrated in their kind invitation, you will not attend. You can even punctuate this with a clever "hashtag," as they like to say. Something on the order of #lazycheapbuttfriend.

So, no, you don't need to decline this "invitation" with your finest vellum monogrammed stationery and fountain pen. It would be high-larious, though, if you did. I mean, if you had the time, think of how perplexed the recipients would be to receive a proper note of regret in their real mailbox. They'd be all like, "Whaaa? I just wanted to know if she wanted to come to my home jewelry party three states away, and, whoa, look at this monogram and shit. . . ."

Question: Isn't it kind of dumb to let the whole world know you're not at home? If you post about your vacay every day on Facebook, couldn't the wrong people find out that you're out of town and go break into your home and steal all your belongings?

Whoa. Someone's been watching too many episodes of *CSI: Fort Wayne* or some such. Actually, you make a good point. I suggest that if you must post real-time updates on your fabulous vacation, beginning with the obligatory picture of your toes in the foreground and the ocean in the background and caption a simple "Ahhhh," then do leave behind a very large and very hungry attack dog for the unfortunate robbers to deal with.

This brings us to, in a roundabout way, the subject of bragging on Facebook. It's extremely poor manners to brag in person, and it's no different in the virtual world. We know that you're over the moon that your up-to-now simpleton of a son hasn't made higher than a D-plus on math and now he's gone and gotten himself a B, but we just don't care. We may "Like" that status, but we're just doing it out of sheer politeness. We don't wish you any ill will, but if your status repeatedly contains phrases like "I'm so proud of my son/daughter/husband/ ferret," you're going to be unfriended. You are a blowhard.

Look, the Princess does plenty of stuff that I never talk about because, at the end of the day, I know that (1) it sounds braggy, and (2) nobody but her parents and closest relatives give a shit. That's the smell test for this stuff. Every time you find your fingers wanting to bang out a quick status update that "Donnie Jr. had the highest grade on the spelling test!" know that your friends think that's kinda douchey. Actually, very douchey.

Even Donnie Jr. thinks so. And he's fairly certain I misspelled douchey.

Question: I'm not sure how I feel about Facebook's If I Die *app*. It seems kinda morbid and creepy to actually leave behind statuses for your friends to upload after you die.

Did I not just tell you that I don't like the word "app" unless it involves gooey melted cheese? I didn't? Well, I meant to. That aside, I agree that it's creepy, though not necessarily a question of etiquette. One of the benefits of being dead should be that you no longer have to fret about shrimp forks and thank-you notes and all the stuff that the mortal world has to deal with every day. No, no. You should be safely ensconced on your puffy white cloud with your only worry that white was never your best color and now here you have to wear it for, like, eternity.

The question is a good one: Is it good manners to speak to people when you're technically dead? The answer? Yes and no. The way this works is that you approve three "trustees" to post your posthumous message(s). This prevents hackery such as the vengeful ex-spouse pretending you're dead and, really, you're fine but on your honeymoon with the new guy, probably posting obnoxious pictures of your toes in the foreground. So, it's nice that there are safeguards in place. Your friends will know when they get your status update that you are, in fact, dead as a mackerel.

I'd say that it's mannersome indeed to leave behind a brief, kind message for those who knew and loved you.

If it's more on the order of the old "I told y'all I didn't feel good," well, that's a bit lazy, now, isn't it? Hence the "yes and no" response.

Remember that fabulous old movie, *My Life,* in which the dying dad, played by Michael Keaton, records a video chock-full of fatherly advice for his kid so that, after he's gone, the kid can still have input from his dad? I always thought that was kind of sweet.

Look, we're all going to die, so we might as well cobble together a message of comfort and joy for friends and family. It'll make them feel good, and what could possibly be more mannerly than that?

Here are some posthumous status-update ideas to help you get started. . . .

Advice for the living:

- Never buy cheap ice cream. Seriously, it's so worth it to spend the extra money. Trust me; I got no dog in this fight anymore, so why would I lie about this?

- Read the classics. I did, and now I'm dead. On second thought, read whatever the hell you want. And watch more TV. They don't talk a lot about Nathaniel Hawthorne up here, but *Duck Dynasty*? All the time. Seriously. I couldn't believe it either.

- Don't smoke. Maybe a little weed now and again to take the edge off , but not cigarettes. The doctors told me that smoking was a "major contributing factor" in my "stage 4 lung cancer" and now I'm "dead" and missing the Super Bowl because the rest of the cloud wanted to watch *Downton Abbey* on PBS. Wait a minute. Maybe this is hell. The cloud thing had me fooled for a minute. . . .

- Treat others as you want to be treated. Simple, old-school golden rule stuff, right? But it's so true, living people.

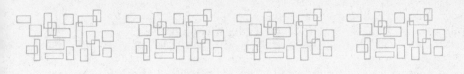

chapter 20

Annoying Chatfest on Aisle Five:
Common Manners Mishaps
at the Grocery Store

The Hungry-Man frozen Salisbury steak dinner with mashed potatoes and fudgy brownie was squished between two jumbo packs of toilet tissue. Alone. Abandoned. Cut from the herd and left to drip to death in a very weird place.

I'm not saying it needed a Sarah McLachlan soundtrack, but it was a sad sight sitting there all soggy and wasteful just because somebody was too much of an assweasel to put it back in the freezer after deciding not to buy it.

Even normally well-mannered people drop all pretense at the grocery store, where those of us who are high-strung, or under ten, behave worst of all.

My least-favorite grocery store memory happened many

years ago as I witnessed a boy who looked about four years
old scream at his exhausted mother: "I hate you, I hate you,
and I'll *always* hate you!" It was chilling, and not just because
we were standing at the freezer case, where her offense was
to deny him the largest pack of freezer pops. I've often wondered what became of little "Damien" since that day at the
A&P so many years ago. I only hope it didn't involve teleki-
netically nudging the nanny out of a fourth-story window to
her death.

**Question: My kids go with me to the grocery store all
the time. How can I get them to stop misbehaving (running around the store, knocking over displays, screaming, and so forth)?**

Most of us resort to bribery. You promise the kids a treat if
they can act less turdlike long enough for you to get everything on your list and back to the car. That said, it sounds like
your kids are committed to making your shopping trip—and
everyone else's—a nightmare. For some reason, this seems to
be less of a problem with the homeschooled families. Their
kids always behave well at the grocery, perhaps out of fear that
if they don't, they'll have to spend time out in the grain silo or
wherever the hell these people really put their kids all day.

Worst kid-in-grocery-store behavior ever: My friend Jana
was in the produce section not long ago when she saw a kid

about nine years old licking the grapes and apples, looking around to see if anybody saw him do it, and then putting them back. Because Jana is a mother herself, she yelled at the kid: "Hey! What the hell do you think you are doing?" At this point, the kid's mom, who has been off to the side—buying fruit that hasn't been licked by someone's child—asks what's going on, and Jana told her that her son was licking the fruit and putting it back on the display.

"Hmm. Well, that's weird," says the mom. "Wonder why he's doing that? Oh, well. What're you gonna do? Kids!"

Yes! Kids! What're you gonna do? I dunno ... leave his fruit-lickin' ass home next time? Yeah, that works.

Back to the original question, though. If bribery doesn't work, you have to leave them home until they're old enough to behave because, and I mean this from the bottom of my heart, you and your brood are shaving years off my life. I have bruises from your insufferable spawn pushing your cart into my shins and a monster headache from all that screaming. Just remember: Contraception is not just a city in South America.

Question: Why do people move so slowly in the grocery store aisles? It's as if they've been drugged!

I know, right? The grocery store is the native habitat of the genus *Saunteringus malingerus*. Keep the grocery cart in a forward motion, people. Do not amble along, blocking the aisles so you can gaze longingly at that Duncan Hines molten lava cake mix. I mean, I get that it looks awesome, but pull to the side, just as you would on the road. No, stupid. The right side. Grocery cart rules are the same as road rules: Stay to the right and don't just park in the middle of the "roadway" and walk away. If you're going to be gone for a while, tie a white paper towel to your cart.

I used to think that it was just me who suffered from grocery store–induced "slow-walker rage," but according to the *Wall Street Journal,* there are fifteen thousand members and counting in a Facebook group called "I Secretly Want to Punch Slow Walking People in the Back of the Head." Like-likelikelikelike.

Question: What do you think of these "extreme coupon" people who go to the checkout lane with two full carts and a coupon for every item? They tie up the cashier forever. Isn't that poor etiquette?

These people kinda freak me out, if you must know. They're hoarding hundreds of cans of Manwich in their garages, pallets of Lucky Charms under their beds, and tubs full of Brawny towels in their guest baths.

The problem is that it's hard to talk about them without coming across as elitist, out of touch, or even a little jealous of their mad couponing skills. Which I am none of these things. You can't be elitist if you're honestly upset that somebody's hoarding the Manwich, right?

If you're giving a lot of your coupon megabuys to charity, then good on you. If you're laid off and this is the only way you can make ends meet, then double good on you. But those who do it just for the thrill of buying two carts piled high with Right Guard for a nickel or so much Cottonelle that you have to back both cars out of the garage, well, you might have a problem. You don't want to end up on *Hoarders, Hoarding: Buried Alive, The Hoard Monsters* or *Hoarding Wars, The Passion of the Hoarders* or *Bayou Catfishing Hoarders Who Have Storage and Parking Wars* or some such.

I get that it's kind of a rush. And while I think it's cute that an extreme-coupon mom might teach her toddler how to count to one thousand by making him inventory the mac-'n'-cheese boxes in his bedroom closet, shouldn't he be outside in the sunshine, blowing bubbles or something?

Bottom line: Anything that inconveniences others to a great degree is always an etiquette violation. I would hope that these extreme types shop in the off-hours. If it's 5:30 P.M., and you whip out a three-inch binder with plastic sleeves full of coupons for the 850 items in your cart to be individually scanned, I will go all Charlie Sheen on you. I mean the old Charlie Sheen who scared everybody a little, not the mellow, neutered version nobody much cares about.

Question: I can't stand being in the grocery store and hearing some idiot on a cell phone describe every single thing on the shelves. What's up with that?

Stop calling my husband an idiot. On his annual trip because I have anthrax or something, he'll call precisely eighteen times to make sure he gets the right thing. It would be endearing if it wasn't so craptastically annoying.

"Hmmm. I see Minestrone, Cream of Chicken, Beef Barley, Chicken and Stars . . ."

At the oatmeal aisle, he calls to tell me there's "thick and rough, Irish, steel-cut, extra thick, rolled and organic with flaxseed, apple-tastic, one-minute, five-minute, cinnamon, weight control with fiber, heart medley, strawberry cream, oat revolution . . ."

Tip: Keep your list very specific if you send someone to the grocery store who is unfamiliar with the layout. I have a friend who, in utter desperation, sent her husband to the grocery for Eagle Brand milk. He spent two hours in dairy before he finally asked for help. By the time he was steered to the baking section, home of the *canned* milk, he was a whimpering mess. "Milk. In cans? How?" is pretty much all he could say.

Question: Why do so many shoppers think that it's okay to block the grocery store aisles while they have a very long conversation with a friend or neighbor?

I know what you mean. One time, I actually got the stink eye from two women who were visibly pissed that I'd interrupted their utterly fascinating conversation to ask them to move the hell out of the way so I could get to the Lean Cuisines. They were all, like, "I can't believe how rude that was," and I was all, like, "Tha's right, bitches; shit just got *real!*"

Okay, that didn't happen beyond the part about the stink eye, which I did get when I simply said, "Excuse me, please," forcing them to suspend their conversation, which involved a lot of one-up-yoursmanship as they compared their adult sons' careers, lives, and families long enough for me to retrieve my 350-calorie Mandarin chicken. Which rocks, by the way.

It would be a wonderful world if you could just get a running start and use your cart to slam into 'em like a bowling ball scattering pins, but that would be a huge violation of etiquette. Fun as hell, though.

Soup to Nuts . . .

- You know they make those freezer doors out of clear glass so you don't have to open them and stand there and stare, letting all the food defrost. Don't be a dick; look at the food through the glass door, make your selection, open the door quickly, retrieve the food; close the door. See how easy?

- A word about the U-Scan. Usually there are two banks of these serve-yourself checkouts. Do you queue up on one side, or do you simply hover in the middle and grab the first one available? I prefer the latter choice because it's a bit of a free-for-all in there, isn't it? If you hover in the middle, you block both, thus assuring that you will have the first-available scanner. You're welcome.

- Don't try to feed your entire family at those little food stations that show up in grocery stores on weekends or at warehouse clubs like Costco every day. Take one sample per station if you must, and make sure the kids don't bogart all the frozen chocolate banana samples. Those are for *my* kid. By the way, I must warn you that it's not a good idea to try all the samples, for one very practical reason. I once fell quite ill after mixing the frozen shrimp rolls with the portobello ravioli with the mini-calzones with the marshmallow trail mix with the spinach dip with the cheesy chicken loaf. . . . Just because it's there and there's a nice woman making it sound like that frozen hot dog and tortilla soup is going to change your life (it won't), you don't have to partake. Use discretion. Oh, and don't throw your toothpicks on the floor or, alternately, chew on them the rest of the day. That's nasty.

- Put the damn cart back in the corral. Is it really that hard to do this? It must be, judging from all the grocery carts I see abandoned all over the parking lot. Sometimes it's hard to park the car because Leonard P. Superdouche has just shoved the cart into a space instead of returning it to the corral just a few feet away.

- A quick reminder: Don't act surprised when it's time to pay the cashier. Have your loyal customer card ready. Ditto your debit card. Oh, and if you're still writing checks to pay for your groceries, please return home immediately. 1997 is calling.

- Don't you dare crowd me while I'm still waiting for my transaction to be completed. I've actually had to say, "Do you mind?" to a creeper. If you hover, I promise I will just go slower to piss you off.

chapter 21

Criminal Misconduct: How to Behave When Being Arrested

Yes, even when breaking the law (or, in my case, being wrongfully accused of breaking the law—more on that later), it's important to show that you were "raised right."

When I read about how even the Amish—*the Amish*—were misbehaving and breaking laws of civility, well, I nearly threw in the etiquette towel (which is made of painstakingly embroidered Egyptian cotton, it should be noted).

When the Amish—a gentle people known for finely crafted furniture and inventing a stove that claims to heat your home for about thirty-seven cents a winter—start showing signs of misbehavior it really sets one back a bit.

It turns out that the Amish have something akin to rival gangs terrorizing one another in rural Ohio.

Where, oh, where are the mannersome men that Aunt Verlie raved about meeting on her church bus trip to Amish Country? A land where piecrusts don't come frozen in foil pans? Where it's a sin to boast about the quality of one's apple butter? Where tourists learn to build their own "Amish friend" from wood scraps. Yes! All that and only thirty minutes from the nearest Tanger Outlets. Heaven!

But now, the Amish, long insulated from the wretched excesses of American culture (zippers! cars! HBO!) have finally snapped and joined the rest of us in repudiating common courtesy. Big-time.

Behaving like a button-flied version of Bloods and Crips, the Amish of Ohio are giving new meaning to the phrase "crazy quilt," as they break into one another's homes and clip one another's beards off.

What's next? Carving gang symbols in the cornfield? The keying of buggies? The tipping of butter churns or (gasp!) accusations of "Thine mama!"

Of course, not all Amish are acting this way. Just a splinter group of really pissed-off Amish who believe the enemy isn't Amish enough. Night-lights on buggies? Heresy!

The majority remain well-mannered and orderly, leading peaceful iPad-free lives. But those rogue Amish? They are harbingers of things to come. For, verily, when the Amish "act ugly," we imagine it will only be a short leap until the Jehovah's Witnesses will not just show up in Sunday clothes at your door at o'-dark-thirty on Saturday morning with pamphlets. No, these perennially lovely and well-mannered folk will egg your house if you don't answer. Could happen.

Now, as for my own brush with the law, let me just say that it's very, very important to be more polite than usual when dealing with the police.

Politeness pays off hugely when pulled over (wrongfully!) by the officer with the blue light.

The light came out of nowhere, as they always do.

"Mommy, I think he wants you to stop," said the Princess.

"Nonsense, dear," I said. "He's probably after some miscreant. So many idiots can't drive in this town."

And, yes, I did say "miscreant."

I had to admit it was odd how even though I traveled several blocks, he insisted on staying close (really, too close) with that silly light on.

I turned onto our street and *he did, too*!

He then motioned me to roll down the window and asked for my license and registration.

I behaved as I always do in this kind of situation: as though I had a ton of weed and a bunch of illegal aliens in my trunk.

The Princess was staring straight ahead, pretty much stuck between "mortifed" and "scarred for life."

"Do you know why I stopped you?" the officer asked.

I remembered my friend Elle, who was so nervous when

she got pulled over that she answered the same question with "No, Your Majesty!"

"Uhhhh, no, sir, Officer, sir, no disrespect intended, sir, but no, no clue here. Respect." I sounded like Ali G.

He said I ran a red light.

I most certainly did not. The Princess would back me up on that.

"Tell him! I would never run a red light with you in the car. Or just me. Or anyone! Never!"

The Princess just shrugged. "I wasn't looking. Sorry."

What the *what*?

Several minutes of groveling went on, in which I heard myself swear "on my Tivo and everything that's season-passed on it" if he would just give me a warning ticket.

Which he did.

"Thank you, Officer! You *rock*!" I said while the Princess slumped farther down in her seat. Just like a miscreant.

As you can see, politeness was the key here. I treated him with the utmost respect. Also, I was completely innocent.

Now, for the flip side, consider the extraordinary poor etiquette demonstrated by an Ohio schoolteacher (what's in the water in Ohio lately?) who was arrested after she sprayed sheriff's deputies with breast milk when they tried to remove her from a car.

The teacher, thirty, and apparently lactating to beat the band, was attending a wedding reception when she got likkered up, had a big fight with her hubby, and locked herself in their car.

When the cops tried to remove her, she advised them that she was "a breast-feeding mother." This is usually an idle threat that I only employed one time to get ahead in line at Target. It went unsaid that if I didn't get to my baby soon, my breasts would explode all over the Doritos end cap, and nobody wanted to see that.

But "Ohio" made good on her threat and doused the deputies with a breastly weapon, as it were. She also sprayed their car with her breast milk, calling to mind those wands at the self-service car wash that can be set on "suds" or "prewax."

I have a grudging, weird respect for this woman who had no resources to fight "the man" except what she could come up with on her own chest. In a way, it was the ultimate MacGyver moment, except that MacGyver never had breasts, and if he did, he would've used them only to defeat true evil, not hose down some well-intentioned Midwestern cops. What do you think they told her? "Put your hands up and your tits down?"

On the other hand—woman, please. You know how people get all nervous about breast-feeding. How many times have we seen protesters picketing restaurants and malls where breast-feeding is banned? I've never gotten how some grown-ups could be threatened by such a natural act of simple nutrition, but then I don't get how some grown-ups could think that Michele Bachmann would make a better president than, say, a rutabaga.

The Ohio sheriff who investigated and milked the moment, so to speak, was a master of understatement when he said, "This is a prime example of how alcohol can make individuals do things that they would not normally do."

You think?

Alcohol does enable all sorts of bad behavior. Just look at those mug shot magazines, and you can always tell that many of the accused are wasted. Some are baked, but most are wasted. It's a fine distinction.

Either way, it's rude to be drunk in public. And even ruder, still, to be arrested and photographed with a big sloppy grin on your face. Getting arrested is a solemn event, and your mug shot should reflect that.

My girlfriends are addicted to these mug shot magazines and love the "frequent fliers," who mug for the camera like they're at a social event.

Do these criminals keep an album of their mug shots to be shared with friends and family? "Lookit, here's where I face-planted on that sidewalk downtown 'cause of too much tequila. Again."

Also, and I really can't stress this enough, if you are going to lead a life of crime, don't commit the error in judgment demonstrated by one mug shot magazine star. The one with the Olde English tattoo reading *Fuck the Law!* scrolling

across his forehead. At this point, I can only give him one
word of advice: bangs.

**Question: I hate to admit it, but I'm addicted to those
mug shot magazines like Cuffed. Why do so many
people read this junk?**

Sorry, what? I was just at the convenience store, and I don't
know about y'all but I like a little drunked-up prostitute mug
shot with my gas fill-up and strawberry Mentos.

It's America's pastime, and it might very well bring families together. My friend likes to play the mug shot game with
her teenagers, matching the face with the crime. Meth addicts
are easy to spot with their sunken cheeks and bad teeth.

"This is a teachable moment," said Brandi Sue (not her real
name because, well, she'd kick my ass). "It's important to see
what can happen when you do drugs like meth. Thousands
of dollars in orthodontia wasted like that? Now, that would be
a crime."

**Question: I always look at the mug shots on my news-
paper's Web site, and recently I spotted a mug shot of
my next-door neighbor. This is awkward because it
was for assault. Should I act like I don't know?**

Well, he could be innocent, you know. It's possible he was
provoked into responding in an unmannerly way to defend

someone's honor. I know. I crack myself up. Of course he's guilty. Give him a wide berth at the neighborhood potluck. You don't want to get him riled by asking him to "pass the ah-salt" or some such. Tempting though it is to just give in to the easy pun.

Just the Facts, Ma'am

- Be respectful when stopped for a traffic violation, no matter how idiotic it seems at the time.
- Never use your breasts as a weapon. Use them as God intended, to wangle your way into the rave for free.
- Do not smile in a mug shot. It makes you look like kind of a dick.

chapter 22

*

Gossip Girl:
How to Steer the Conversation to Higher
Ground Without Pissing Everybody Off

You remember the game Telephone? It's the one where you'd whisper a message into a kid's ear and then they'd whisper it—just once—to the kid beside them and so it went around the room. It was an easy kids' party game back in the day and usually good for a laugh when you heard how much the original message had changed by the time it went through a bunch of little ears. Thus: "We're going to have strawberry birthday cake in ten minutes" morphed into "We're going to crawl behind the lake with ten midgets."

I felt like I had been at the end of that game when I recently repeated to several friends that I heard that Martha Stewart's daughter, Alexis, wrote in her book that Martha routinely pees on the bathroom floor.

In fact, Alexis Stewart's "tell all" actually reported that Martha sometimes peed with the bathroom door open.

Which is a hell of a lot less interesting than my version. I didn't mean to spread gossip; it's just that I heard a review of the book on National Smart Person Radio and was paying only a little bit of attention.

So, to anyone I told that Martha Stewart pees on the floor, I was wrong. And to Martha, I apologize.

The point of all this is that Alexis Stewart is kind of a bitch.

No, sorry, that wasn't the point, although I do suspect it's true. The point is that gossip is usually false, often hurtful, and always bad manners.

I've noticed that, over the past couple of years, I've stopped gossiping as much as I used to. This has led my friends to say things like, "Wow, you sure aren't as interesting as you used to be" and "You know stuff but you're not sharing and it's starting to freak us out."

Sadly, they're right. Gossip, like the perfect vodka martini, just makes everyone more interesting. But the truth is, I'm getting too old for this stuff and I'm tired of being gossip's bitch.

I didn't stop gossiping overnight. I didn't even do it consciously. It's just that one day, I woke up and realized that I was pausing ever so briefly before I casually trashed somebody's character. Sometimes the pause was so long, it never even happened. I know; scary, right?

Now, you should know that this new gossip avoidance is just for real people, not actors, politicians, and the like. I am *all in* on spreading malicious gossip about malodorous celebrities. I don't even feel guilty about it, because you know people like Kim Kardashian—who will go so far as to get married just for the publicity and millions of dollars in product endorsements—deserve what they get. Let me be clear: When I say we need to stop gossiping, I'm talking about Regular People, here.

That's why I feel free to talk about Alexis Stewart, who complained that she grew up with a "glue gun pointed at my head." Too bad it wasn't her mouth.

Because I hope to be famous one day, I immediately summoned the Princess to my office and asked her if she planned to write a gossipy tell-all about me one day.

"Who would buy it?" she asked.

"Okay, good point. But still. I just want to make sure you don't have any horrible bits of gossip that you'll share like Alexis Stewart did. Sharper than a serpent's tooth is an ungrateful child. I believe Martin Sheen said that."

After seeing her puzzled look, I explained who Alexis was: a whiny, spoiled Manhattan rich lady who had accomplished nothing without her mother's help and financial backing.

"That sounds a little one-sided," mused the Princess.

And a little child shall lead them. . . .

Question: I don't gossip, but I listen in when others do. If I don't repeat it, then I'm all good in the karma department, right?

Not really. The true stand-up move would be to hold up your hand and say: "Stop right there, Cissy Rae. I don't want to hear anything bad about Bobbie Jean, because I don't think it's nice to spread stories about people."

When steering the convo away from malicious gossip, you want to avoid sounding sanctimonious and judgmental so it's better to just change the subject to something that involves less character assassination and more fashion and pop culture. You can have a delightful girls' night out just with those topics alone. Fill in with genuinely caring questions about somebody's dotty old relative, and you'll leave the table feeling like a better person, I promise. Sweet tea? Yes, please. Hater-ade? Pass.

There is one exception to your new no-gossip policy that is universally approved: If the subject of the gossip is your ex (I mean a serious ex, someone you've either been married to or shacked with) who "done you wrong," well, yes, pull up a chair and enjoy a slander cocktail with a chaser of venom.

Seriously, why should you be the only one who knows he has only one testicle?

Question: What if I'm not gutsy enough to call someone out for spreading gossip? Is there an easier way

to deal with this without alienating everyone at the table?

Silence is your friend. While the others are trashing away, you can simply keep your mouth shut except to sip and nibble. After a while, someone at the table will notice this and say, "You're awfully quiet, Misti Dawn. What's wrong?"

At this point, you can simply say, "Oh, nothing. I was just hoping we could talk about . . ."

They'll know what you're doing, but you've done it in a subtle way that lets everyone off the hook.

Sometimes you can make your point gently. The other night, I was having dinner with some close women friends who began to say some pretty nasty things about a mutual friend. I just said, "She's never acted like that around me. In fact, she's always been extremely kind to everybody, as far as I've seen."

Standing up for someone who really doesn't deserve to be trashed will elevate the entire conversation. When I said that, another woman at the table said, "You know, you're right. She's never done anything like that before. This is probably not even true. . . ."

Question: My best friend is a horrible gossip. Every time we go out, she points to someone and starts telling me how they cheat on their spouse, lie about their income, brag incessantly about their children, et cetera. Then, when the person walks over with a friendly greeting, my friend positively lights up and is super nice to this person she just spent ten minutes defaming. What's up?

What's up is that you can believe with absolute certainty that when your best friend has lunch with another friend next week, she will be throwing *you* under the bus. It will be something along the lines of how you don't love your husband, your kids dress funny and have a "thrown away" look, and—what else? Oh, yes, did she know that you had an abortion in high school? What? You thought you could trust her? Don't make me laugh.

I have an acquaintance who does this routinely, and it's a sight to behold. After skewering a colleague from her workplace for a good hour, she lavished air kisses on the same colleague that very night at a formal event and went on and on about how pretty she looked.

My advice? Give people like this a very wide berth. They are unrepentant low-road assholes. And that's not gossip; that's fact. Hypocrisy is always bad manners.

Question: My daughter goes to a dance studio where the kids are extremely competitive. Some of the dance moms like to drop little snide remarks that aren't even true to make their kid seem better. For instance, they gossip about the oldest girl having sex or how one of the girls is a lesbian. I'd confront them about all the malicious gossip, but I think they'd eat me.

Ah, yes, the dance mom. Having been one for twelve years now, I know of what you speak. While I've never observed the kind of horror you see on Lifetime's *Dance Moms* reality show, I don't doubt that it exists in the real world. Today, the Princess attends a kinder, gentler studio where the students genuinely support one another, and the moms stay in their cars in the parking lot, where they belong. No one's going to bring home a five-foot-tall trophy (and where the hell would you put it, anyway?), but she's learning a lot. My advice is to pick your studio carefully. Get away from that toxic dump of a dance school and find a better match.

Question: Do you ever miss those really juicy, down-and-dirty, not-a-smidgen-of-truth-to-any-of-it gossip sessions with your friends? Isn't life on the high road a little dull?

Yes and yes. But I swear to you, as corny as it sounds, I sleep better at night and I like myself more in the morning, now that I'm not gossiping about real people. As much.

There were times when the gossip was so vile that I felt like I needed a *Silkwood* shower (ask your parents) when I got home from a night out, but I don't feel that way anymore.

Well, not usually. Naturally, I backslide occasionally, but the slips are coming less often, I promise.

As Southerners, we are taught to embrace that famous line from *Steel Magnolias*: "If you can't say anything nice about anybody, come sit by me."

It's hilarious every time to me, still. And what of the tenderly held belief, taught from the cradle, that it's okay to say any awful thing about someone as long as you preface it with a "bless her heart" or "bless his heart"?

Have I turned my back on my Southerness? Of course not. I've just been doing a little fine-tuning, is all. Bless my heart.

chapter 23

Space, the Final Frontier:

How to Get Some,

How to Give Some

The well-dressed woman at the neighborhood Christmas party approached with a warm smile. Despite her friendly demeanor, I instinctively tensed up. She's someone I know in only the most casual way. Our daughters are roughly the same age and we have a few mutual friends. She's friendly; oh, precious Lord, is she friendly. She is, in *Seinfeld*-speak, a "low-talker." She seems to know this about herself, and perhaps this is why she is also a "close-talker." She can't seem to help herself.

She approached to say hello, and before I knew it, our faces were exactly three inches apart. When she laughed, I could see a tiny residue of Goldfish cracker bobbing up and down on her uvula.

Now, it should be stated that this close-talker has marvelous breath, so that's not an issue. No odor, just the sensation

of a wind gust as she forces the words out in a disconcert-
ingly sexy half whisper.

I have no idea what "CT" is saying because by now, I am,
quite literally, against the wall, head back at a ninety-degree
angle, while she maintains the three-inch distance. It's face
rape.

She continues chatting and laughing while I just nod my
head up and down, excruciatingly aware that if I open my
mouth, she will realize that I have spent way too much time
with the garlic dip.

Finally, Duh Hubby realizes that I have been face-pinned
by this repeat offender and walks over to rescue me. She immediately shifts her gaze and close-talks him while I smile,
skip away, and head back to my own kind at the dip table.

Close-talkers and people unaware of the rules of Personal
Space aren't doing this to aggravate us. They simply don't know
any better. Perhaps it's a genetic problem. For all I know, this
otherwise lovely and impeccably mannered woman comes
from a long line of close-talkers and hoverers. I picture her
sturdy pioneer ancestors hoeing a field, all working within
about four inches of one another. They probably made shitty
farmers.

There is simply no polite way to deal with a close-talker.
You can't very well tell them what you're thinking: *"Back off!
You're freaking me out!"* No, the only true solution is Vigilant
Avoidance. As soon as she or he approaches, gives the "I'm
coming for you" wave, and heads in your direction, just knock

over a couple of chairs and make your escape, just like in the movies. Apologize to the host for the broken furniture in a lovely note the next day.

I'm kidding, of course. No need for a note, because you'll never be invited back after making that nasty little scene. Vigilant Avoidance just means you very discreetly slip away after returning a friendly wave.

Close-talkers are the most serious violators of personal space, but there are plenty of others. You know who you are.

Question: I'm not a hugger. Don't get me wrong; I'm not gonna go all Temple Grandin on you if you try it. It's just that I think that casual hugging is unnecessary and awkward. Last night was the final straw. My husband introduced me to his boss's wife, and she flung her arms wide and I realized I was expected to respond. I don't even **know** *this woman. Isn't this kind of forced intimacy inappropriate? Will she expect me to do the "hug and air kiss" combo next time? I could hardly rebuff her because, as I mentioned, she is my husband's boss's wife. But I was extremely put off by the whole thing.*

You sure do belabor a point. Right now, I'd rather slug you than hug you. Do you ever shut up? Didn't think so.

Your yammering aside, the problem of unsolicited hugging is a huge one. I mean it's not up there with famine in Darfur, but it's big. This is, I suppose, what some might snarkily place under the heading of "rich people problems." (Ooooh, she doesn't like to be hugged. How terrible for her. How she must suffer day after day just because some well-meaning human puppy wants to communicate friendliness. Beats the real-puppy way, which involves sniffing your ass, so be grateful for that, at least.)

But, really, unsolicited hugging is a problem, and I am sympathetic. So here's what you do. Before you can be tackled by a virtual stranger, stick your hand out for a friendly, firm handshake with a duration of two to three seconds, no more. When combined with a toothy smile and a "So nice to meet you, Biff!" it won't appear hostile.

Now, you should know there's a chance this will be taken as an invitation to pull you forward using your "just for shaking" hand and, yes, you'll be hugged. If this happens, try not to visibly recoil. Lookit: Some people are huggers and others aren't. If it truly makes you uncomfortable, maybe you shouldn't accept social invitations at all and you should, instead, sit around in your Forever Lazy swaddling clothes, watching *Law & Order: SVU* marathons. Or as I like to call it: Monday–Friday.

Question: Why do people stand so far apart in fast-food lines? It's not the ATM, for Pete's sake.

This question (on a subject about which I've been a bit fanatical over the years) illustrates how it's also possible to violate personal space by being too far apart. Let me put this simply: The guy ahead of you in line at McDonald's isn't trying to ask the order-taker for a blow job. I mean, I hope. He's also not sharing his social security number, Iran's nuclear secrets, his HIV status, or anything else private and personal. Rather, he is ordering "the number five and two apple turnovers." So cozy up a bit so the rest of us don't have to queue up in the parking lot, where the seagulls can shit on our heads and the guy with the cardboard GOD BLESS sign won't make us feel so dreadfully guilty for not contributing to his malt likker fund at eleven in the morning.

Question: I've heard that in Europe people often share tables in a communal fashion. The other day, two total strangers sat at the empty two seats at my lunch table in a crowded diner. They didn't ask or anything. Were they European?

Hmmm. I don't know. Were they smoking? Did they have their dogs with them? Did they smell a bit, uh, ripe? How many other offensive stereotypes can I summon to answer your pea-headed question?

That said, I realize that it can be unsettling for those of us with personal-space issues to suddenly be joined by strangers from foreign countries while we're trying to eat our falafel and baba ghanoush, for God's sake. To some people, the communal table provides a wonderful opportunity to meet someone new and, perhaps, strike up a conversation or even a potential friendship. These are the same people who happily sign up to host foreign exchange students in their homes. Commendable but completely weird. Whenever my sweet friend Dana asks if I would consider hosting one of her Vietnamese exchange students, I always remind her that I can't do this because I refuse to spend an entire school year unable to fart out loud in my own home. I can't believe she forgets this every year.

While I admire these openhearted friendly folks like Dana, I am a True American. Which means that I have zero interest in learning about another culture unless it is in the safe confines of Epcot or the International House of Pancakes.

What to do? I find it useful to block off potential table-sharers by placing my huge movie-popcorn purse in front of me. You can also add scattered papers, leaflets, your noose collection, anything large and unwieldy to form a visual barricade. If someone approaches and asks if they may use the empty chairs at another table, say yes immediately. Crisis averted.

Question: What about the subway? Is there a way to maintain acceptable personal space in such tight quarters?

I read somewhere recently that some Amish sects bathe only once a week. You could go that route, but please don't. I have ridden subways to ballgames at Wrigley Field, Fenway Park, and Yankee Stadium. This is the most crowded subway experience anyone could possibly endure, and I am fairly certain that the Chicago train resulted in at least one of my orifices being violated by a foam finger. To say that we were packed in like sardines is a disservice to sardines everywhere. The only solution: Never ride the subway during peak times and with peak destinations using so-called express trains. You might not make any stops along the way, but you will feel another's heartbeat for the first time since you were pregnant. It doesn't help that, this time around, the heartbeat belongs to that same guy with the GOD BLESS sign.

Question: My husband gave me a gift certificate for a massage at a really nice spa. I don't have the heart to tell him that I don't like the idea of strangers touching me, even therapeutically.

Okay, you're what they call an outlier. That means you're out there lying about this whole thing. You know you want a nice massage because it will make you feel all warm and gooshy inside. It's like slamming back a few single malt Scotches but without the hangover. If it's a reputable spa, they know to place sheets and towels to cover your naughties, so no worries there. I would, however, steer away from a growing cadre of "freelance" massage therapists like the one I just saw driving a shitty-looking gray van with LET ME COME TO YOUR HOUSE AND MASSAGE U! painted all over the side panels. I pulled up beside this fellow at the stoplight, and he looked a lot like Jeff Bridges's character in *True Grit*. Gray, straggly beard; rheumy eyes; and a chaw in his jaw. Yeah, stay away from that guy.

God bless.

chapter 24

*Wedding Etiquette:
Do's, Don'ts, and
"No, She Did-un'ts"*

L et's cut to the chase, shall we? A lot has happened to the traditional wedding ceremony in the past couple of years. How many YouTube uploads must we see to confirm that much more time is spent choreographing a dance routine starring the entire wedding party than is spent on premarital counseling?

Yes, we get that you always wanted to star in your very own music video, but there's no longer the element of surprise in these "flash mob"–style reception dances. In fact, we barely look up from our soy-ginger chicken wings to watch anymore. If we can wipe off our fingers and summon the energy to record it with our iPhone, we will. Wait. It's "Thriller" again. Never mind.

At the risk of sounding like everyone's Aunt Minerva, I wish couples would put half as much energy and passion into making sure that they're right for one another as they do into these much-rehearsed dance performances. In their minds, I guess marriage begins at the moment of reception.

There, I said it.

Question: We just received the long-awaited video of our daughter's wedding. Upon viewing the DVD, which was made by the best man, my husband and I were absolutely floored by the amount of profanity and hideously vulgar language used by the groomsmen during the part where guests were "interviewed" at the reception. This should be a lovely and lasting memento of a beautiful day, not an obscene party video. What must we do?

Oh, dear. I see one thing that hasn't changed over the years is the role of the best man as the Drunkest Bastard in the Room. Look. He has just lost his bestie, and he's acting out. I'm not saying it excuses his Cecil B. DeCreep video efforts, but you should realize that he's hurting. He's jealous that his best friend has "moved on," "grown up," and left behind the *queso*-encrusted foosball table they shared to spend his weekends wandering the aisles of Ikea with "that bitch"—er, your daughter.

A professional videographer knows to let the drunks rant and then skillfully edits away the unpleasant language—at least in the PG version he presents the parents and in-laws.

When your daughter gets married the next time, hire a pro. What? This is going to be her only marriage? Oh, that is just precious and darling.

Question: My wife and I recently received a wedding invitation that had this note at the bottom: "Please, no boxed gifts." I believe I speak for many others when I respectfully ask, "What the hell?"

This is one of the most egregious violations of wedding etiquette out there. Why not just say what you really mean? "Please don't give us a motherhumpin' toaster oven. We don't have the brains God gave plankton, so we'd never figure out how to use it. Yes, we are that stupid. All we want is some serious chedda so we can take that vacay to Cancún."

This odious tendency to sneakily ask for cash as a wedding gift is multiplying faster than germs in a chocolate fountain. Here in the South, we are highly resistant to this sort of thing because it cheapens the occasion. We already have to worry about the bridal couple dancing an elaborately choreographed version of "Back That Azz Up" and the best man making a complete fool of himself on video, and now . . . this.

If you do relent, and give cash as requested, make sure that you eat the precise value of the cash given at the reception. In other words: prawns, yes; hard rolls, no. Or you can go renegade-badass and give them the biggest chicken rotisserie you can find at Costco. Wrap it up in tacky wedding-bell paper and make a big show of asking, "Where's the gift table?" when you get to the reception.

They'll take it back, of course, but that's their problem. And isn't it fun to think of them fuming about your thoughtlessness and huffing about as they try to fit that bird-turner into their Kia Sportage? Thought so.

Question: It has been nine months since the wedding, and I'm still waiting on a thank-you note. Apparently, a Mixmaster with detachable meat grinder isn't the big deal it used to be! Seriously, why do some couples take so long to say thank you?

Wow! I can assure you that if I got that present, I'd drive to your house with a coolerful of freshly ground homemade sausage to show my undying appreciation. Unfortunately, somewhere along the line, the word got out that it was acceptable for a couple to take up to one year to mail their thank-you notes after the wedding.

This is oft repeated like those scary e-mails you get from idiot friends. Things like how if you soak a human tooth in

Pepsi, it will dissolve overnight. It's bunk, hokum, and completely untrue. Sadly, there is no Snopes for this sort of thing, so we must resort to using our common sense and common decency.

The truth? Thank-you notes should always be sent within three months of receiving the gift. Anything more than that indicates that you have found the whole thank-you thing such a terrible chore that you just can't quite believe you have to do it. Poor you. If you wait more than three months to write your notes and mail them, people will talk bad about you. And they'll do so for way longer than a year.

Question: What's with that guy on TV who has four wives?

Okay, I actually made up that question because I am currently obsessed with TLC's *Sister Wives,* and I'm dying to talk about it. The only thing more challenging than one wedding is four, with four different brides.

Oh, how I love to follow the lives of the smiling puppy-faced Kody Brown, who rotates through his four wives' bedrooms like a Roomba on testosterone. With his moppish blond hair and surprisingly ripped bod, Kody looks and acts like the one guy in the frat house who you always suspected was actually forty-five years old. He giggles behind his hands when he's busted for whatever ticks off four women at a time.

I was expecting the four brides to be dour, hard-faced women obsessed with martyrdom, homeschooling, and those scary-tight polygamy-gal cornrows, but these chicks are downright mouthy. You should've heard them carp about how they didn't get to help bride number four pick out her wedding gown. The nerve!

I get what Kody gets out of the arrangement (he's a man with four sex partners who know about one another, and yet none of them wants to strangle him with piano wire while he's sleeping), but I'm not sure what's in it for the women except they like each other a lot, and I get the feeling they'd be fine without Kody in a *Golden Girls* kind of way. They get along great, which is nice since you-know-who is always hovering outside the bedroom door with his motor running, so to speak.

Kody is like a golden retriever, if a golden retriever had Lumineers and could actually bark out, "It's!" "All!" "Good!" for every situation, from facing felony charges for polygamy to having to pay for four different rental houses. He's not the perfect groom; in truth, he comes off as kind of a dunderhead, but he does seem happy, perhaps because he gets laid a bazillion times a week and never actually does any child care. Cool.

Question: Weddings have become some sort of spectator sport. Look at the proliferation of TV shows like

Say Yes to the Dress *and* Four Weddings. *Whatever happened to the sanctity of marriage?*

That's easy. Kim Kardashian happened to it. For every royal wedding in which we sniffle happy tears to see that William has chosen a lovely, elegant bride who would've been adored by Our Beloved Lady Diana May She Rest in Peace, we are subjected to many more of the common and foul-mouthed, the anal-bleached and the Botoxed.

Kim's marriage to "some basketball player" was made into a two-hour TV special that generated millions in ad revenue. She filed for divorce seventy-two days later, citing "irreconcilable differences." Uh-huh. I suppose this was the day the last check cleared. Call me a sentimental fool, but I would hope that a marriage would last longer than the mustard in my fridge.

If you want to see what's really wrong with weddings today, watch an episode of *Say Yes to the Dress*. No, not the one episode with a conscience, where they're fitting a gown on the paralyzed chick, but the rest of them. My least favorite brides casually drop eighty thousand dollars on a couture wedding gown because they "always wanted to be a princess." Let me be frank: You're a little old for that, Your Hagship. Why not use that money to help out somebody less fortunate because, trust me, a year from now, nobody's going to remember your gown didn't come from the five-hundred-dollar rack at David's Bridal. Nobody.

Question: Why do so many celebrity marriages end so badly?

You mean like Ashton and Demi? As my friend Amy pointed out, that marriage broke down when Demi finally figured out she was married to Kelso. If ever there was a case of arrested development, it was Ashton, who seemed happiest in his role as the shaggy stoner in *That '70s Show*.

There are some who think that the age difference between Ashton and Demi—she's 135 years older than he—was the real reason for the breakup, but I don't think so. I happen to be married to a younger man myself. What's it like, you ask? Well, Duh Hubby finds it extraordinarily amusing to tug on my sleeve every so often and ask, "What was Vietnam really like?"

This sort of "humor" can be the foundation of a solid and satisfying marriage. Or it can be the catalyst for someone to be "hit upside the head," as we say in the South, depending on whether or not I've had my prunes that morning.

I knew the marriage was on the rocks when Ashton gave Demi an eco-friendly Lexus for her birthday. Nothing says, "You're still as sexy as the day I laid eyes on you" like a hybrid sedan that would be more at home in the cafeteria parking lot than cruising the PCH with the wind wildly whipping your extensions.

My humble opinion? Celebrity marriages tend to be short-

lived because they don't understand that there has to be com-
promise and (gasp!) sacrifice in a marriage. The successful
ones (Kevin Bacon and Kyra Sedgwick, or Ben Affleck and
Jennifer Garner, for instance) get that you may have to take
turns being famous for the marriage to thrive. Home fires
burning and all that.

Nuts and Mints

- If anyone ever calls their fiancé "my soul mate," the
  marriage will last no longer than eighteen months.
  Every time.
- Don't fill your wedding party with kids. Lady Louise,
  seven, and Viscount Severn, three, were attendants
  in the wedding of Prince William to Kate Middleton.
  Poor little boy. I'm already picturing the numerous
  swirlies at Royal Pain Academy and invitations by
  burlier classmates to "Viscount this!" As to Lady Louise, why should anyone who is barely old enough to
  recite her "timeses" participate in the most important event of your life? I mean, until the next most
  important one.
- It's not cute to let your dog be the ring bearer. Sure,
  you'll get a chorus of "awwwwws," but at the heart
  of it, you've just given over one of the most profound

moments of the day to a furry fellow who just wants to spend the day licking his own genitalia. Sure, that describes the best man, too, but somehow it's different.

- Brides: Never marry a man who makes significantly less money than you do. Your mother isn't wrong about this, and neither am I.

- Grooms: Never marry a woman who makes significantly less money than you do. Your father isn't wrong about this, and neither am I.

- Be nice to all your guests, even the ones you don't know but had to invite because your mother convinced you that there would be hurt feelings and "You can't put the toothpaste back in the tube once that happens." That's the kind of shit mothers say. Smile, put on a good party face, and think of how pleasant Kate Middleton looked even as she was surely dying to ask Helena Bonham Carter if she ever plans to release the squirrel monkey that is obviously hiding in her hair.

chapter 25

*

Phoning It In:
Does Anybody Know Why That Black Thing
on the Wall Is Ringing?

Oh my God, the weirdest thing just happened. The house phone rang, and *it wasn't my mother.* I saw the caller ID, and it looked like some sort of local number but there was no name attached. The whole thing left me a little shaky, I gotta tell you, so I let it ring until voice mail could pick it up. I mean, really, who actually talks on the phone anymore?

With all the texting and tweeting and Facebook messaging and Tumblring and e-mailing and IM'ing and the rest, I sometimes forget about the old-fashioned phone call. And then I see a *Seinfeld* rerun, and there's Jerry picking up that huge-ass phone with this long *antenna* sticking out of it. He's walking around his apartment all cool, like, "Ha! I live in New York and I have one of those phones you can walk around with inside your home." When he's done, he puts it back in a charger the size of a cat carrier. Too weird.

Nobody uses the phone anymore except your mother and telemarketers or old friends who don't have your cell or can't find you on Facebook.

So, yes, when the landline rings, it's always a bit of a shock. I jump out of my skin just like in that old horror movie where the babysitter answers the phone and that evil voice asks, *"Have you checked the children?"* Yeah, it's just like that.

You know what I really hate? When you answer the phone and someone sounds profoundly disappointed.

"Ohhhhh, I was just going to leave a message," they say with a noticeable pout. "I didn't think you'd actually pick up."

Yes, by all means, forgive the crap out of me for answering a ringing phone in my own home.

These days, I conduct most of my business via text, including texting to make an appointment to talk on the phone (only if absolutely necessary). You can't just call someone out of the blue. If they answered their phone, I wouldn't even know what to say and would probably just ask to speak to their voice mail.

So, yes, I text just like God and the Unlimited Texting Plan from AT&T World Domination intended. Texting eliminates all the useless prattle and chatter. We've got *lives* here, people. Just text your bullshit problem/question/observation to me. Sister Mary Francis.

When I do actually answer the home phone, it's usually with full-on dread and trepidation. Has someone in the family expired? Did I forget to pay the water bill? *What?* Oh, it's just the local public radio station reminding me it's pledge-drive time. It's always pledge-drive time. Those people got more pledge drives than I got hot flashes. It really doesn't go well if they call during a hot flash.

"You can make the pledge online, if you prefer," they say. Oh, no you did-*unt*.

"And you can just e-mail me. Don't call me at this number. I keep this landline for three reasons: Mama, Aunt Verlie, and because I have no idea how to cancel it without mucking up my cable/internet/phone/TiVo package!"

When family does call on "the real phone," as they call it, it's always bad news. Aunt Verlie reports that her sister-in-law has finally gone so dotty that, when nature calls, she starts lifting up her nightgown as soon as she gets out of bed and walks through the house to the bathroom, pulling the gown higher and higher in anticipation of her arrival on the throne. Doesn't care who sees her. Yeah, there's a mental image I can never get rid of.

My handyman sends a text when he's coming over. Ditto the cleaning lady and the yard guy. We're conducting business, here; there is no need for endless conversation. It's fabulous!

I've never been a talk-on-the-phone person but rather one who paces like a caged lioness in flannel pj's when a call lasts over ten minutes, complete with mock stabbing myself in the chest if it's over fifteen minutes.

Dinner plans? Text me. We don't need to talk for thirty minutes when we're going to see each other at night anyway. There won't be anything left to talk about, so we'll sit there, stirring our after-dinner coffee too long and sneaking a peek at our cell phones to check the time.

"You're awfully quiet tonight," a friend says.

Arrrrggggh.

Now, I will admit that it's possible that things have gone too far and that manners have been severely compromised. For instance, just this morning, Duh Hubby was earnestly asking about plans for this evening, and I just held up my hand to stop him and said, "I'll text you the details."

I just didn't have the energy for all that back-and-forth and give-and-take. So, I just texted him a one-sentence description of plans for tonight. Done. Fortunately, Duh likes this trait and has often said that I "think like a man," whatever the hell that means. I think he means it as a compliment because I'm a fan of the quick, short answer and seldom talk about my hair. My hideous, pitifully thin, lifeless hair. What little there is of it. Don't get me started. . . .

Question: I still like the old-fashioned phone call, but all my friends act strangely irritated when I call them and a few of them have even ended the call with a quick, "I'll text you later." I miss the sound of a human voice.

Ha! I hear voices all the time. And they're telling me to tell you that it's 2013. You're old-school and it's charming in a way. Smallpox was old-school, too, but we finally beat that down. We'll beat you down, too.

Question: I am so disgusted by people who rudely answer their cell phones when I'm in the middle of a conversation with them. Another pet peeve? I gave a dinner party recently, and one of the guests texted all the way through dessert. What should I say to people who behave so abominably?

Texting at the table? Are your friends fourteen? I believe that when adults behave this way, you can just say, "Are we disturbing your phone call with our incessant polite dinner party conversation?" Sure, it's like a 12 on the 0–10 bitchiness scale, but that's some tacky shit you just described. The public shaming should work.

As to people who answer a call while you're talking to them in person, guilty as charged. I've even said, "Excuse me, I really have to take this," because, sometimes, you really do have to take this. Cell phones keep us available all the time, and if it's business, sometimes you have to take the call. If you can determine that it's not either work-related or "Shit, I forgot to pick up my kid from gymnastics again"–related, let it go to voice mail. And to those of you who have called me out on this, I apologize. Then again, if you were just a little more interesting, maybe this wouldn't have happened. You might want to work on that.

Question: How do I deal with texts from someone I don't know? It seems like it's happening more frequently lately. Do I respond and say, "I'm not who you think I am?" Do I ignore it?

Funny you should ask. Not long ago, I received a text message that said:

ANY fresh vegetables, for God's sake. Spinach, carrots, lettuce. We R done here!

I have no idea who sent it or why they were so angry about vegetable acquisition, but to use the lingo of the young, it was a classic texting fail.

I texted back:

Wrong recipient.

They texted back:

Sorry.

No harm done, and now that the vegetable rage had been vented, perhaps they could send a more civilized text to the correct recipient.

By the way, texting fails are appallingly common, thanks to the horror that is autocorrect.

DAD:	Your mom and I are going to divorce next month.
DAUGHTER:	WHAT?!? Why??? Call me. Please!!!
DAD:	I wrote Disney and the damn autocorrect changed it. We are going to DISNEY next month.

Question: Is nothing sacred? Every Sunday, at least one cell phone rings during the worship service. Why can't people either turn their phones off or, better still, leave them in their car for one hour?

You are preaching to the choir, my friend. At my church (yes, I go every week; can you think of anyone who needs it more?), it happens all the time and almost always during the pastoral prayer. I can't tell you how unsettling it is to be thoughtfully meditating on the minister's words and suddenly hear that unmistakable classic, "Me So Horny," blast out from a few pews away. Your solution is perfect: Leave the phone in the car. Amen.

Question: I was nearly sideswiped by a guy who was texting while driving. What's the proper etiquette on following him home and beating the living shit out of him with a baseball bat?

While I normally find violent behavior unseemly, this image actually made me tingle with pleasure. It's the same way I feel every time I watch Denzel open up a can of high-tech whup-ass in _Man On Fire,_ the best revenge flick of all time. Truth is, I've had the exact same experience with a texting asshole and was too shaken up to think about revenge at that moment. But now, in the cold light of day, it sounds pretty reasonable to me. Be sure to observe proper "beating the shit out of somebody" etiquette. Introduce yourself, state the reason for your visit, and proceed with caution; that is, making sure there are no witnesses.

Texting while driving is terrifying on many levels. I am forever telling the Princess that if she does that, there will be severe consequences—yes, the worst fate imaginable: She will be forced to sit between her parents at every home basketball game. Shudder!

Question: You know those Bluetooth gizmos? I can't tell when the person in front of me who is wearing one

is talking to me or someone on the phone. It's embarrassing to say "Oh, I'm fine" and realize they weren't even talking to you. What's the etiquette on this annoying accessory?

Bluetooth should be used only when you're in your car and need to talk on the phone, hands-free. It should never remain affixed to your ear in public places like you're Secret Service or some shit. I despise seeing people walking along, talking to themselves like Legitimate Crazy People and then, just as I'm all set to mock them, I see that hateful little blue blinking light. The first time I saw one, I thought it was counting down to when her head was going to explode. Good times.

chapter 26

✳

Overnight Guests:
The Tale of the Screw

I know I cited a skit from *Saturday Night Live* a few chapters back, but there was another recurring bit that illustrated wretched behavior and was called "The Thing That Wouldn't Leave." The "Thing" was the world's most obnoxious guest imaginable, knocking over dainty collectibles, hogging all the food, and in a scene that now seems a bit dated but was hysterically funny at the time, asking, "Mind if I make a few long-distance phone calls?"

Being a good houseguest isn't just good manners; it's good sense if you ever want to be invited back. Don't piss off the college friend who has an oceanfront condo you just love to visit every summer. Make sure that you are the one guest that leaves the place better than you found it. Don't be the Thing That Wouldn't Leave. Benjamin Franklin was right: Fish and houseguests should be tossed after three days. Read on. . . .

Question: When my brother and his family, which includes three kids under ten, come to visit for a week every summer, they act like we are their servants. They never clean up their own messes, and they never even offer to take us out to dinner in exchange for our hospitality. How can we let them know the jig is up?

Your brother is quite the asshat, isn't he? I'm guessing he used to flush your Barbies and put your bra in the freezer? His numbskull wife isn't any better or this wouldn't be happening.

Well, you know what they say about family. You choose your friends but you are saddled with your inconsiderate family members for the rest of your life until one of you dies a slow, withering death in the Times Up! Nursing Home & Rehabilitation Center.

What? That's not what they say? Well. I'm sure it's close.

Your knuckleheaded brother and his family have a good thing going. They drop in for a week to bunk with you and tour the local sights. After a day spent admiring the World's Largest Hairball or some such, they return in time for a lovely dinner and find you deep into a bottle of Three Buck Chuck and brimming with resentment. You, my friend, are a powder keg.

I suggest you go ahead and explode. Tell them the truth: They will never be invited back, ever, until they can help with household chores, keep the place tidy, take you out to dinner or offer to babysit for you at least a couple of nights.

End this ridiculous suffering in silence. He's your brother, not the Dalai Lama. Tell him that it's been real, but if he wants to visit, and he balks at helping out, the local Days Inn is a better option. And, yes, you do realize that "hotels cost money." Man, I'm really starting to hate this guy. . . .

Question: What is my responsibility as a hostess to ferry my houseguests to and from the airport? They don't seem to mind asking me to do so even if their flights are in the wee hours. Why can't they call a taxi?

You know the old saying: You give them an inch, they'll take a yard; you give them a yard, they'll want a swimming pool in it. . . . Some houseguests seem to think that they're entitled to the All-Inclusive Plan. Which is odd, considering you're giving them a free place to stay and, I'm assuming, many meals. As I used to tell the Princess when she was four: "Use your words." Try saying: "That's not convenient, but here's the number to call for a cab."

Oooh, I can just hear those big-girl panties being snapped into place!

Question: Why is it that every time I have a house-guest, this otherwise normal adult seems incapable

of operating a coffeemaker, microwave, et cetera, with-out howling for help. I'm talking about thirty-something professionals here.

I'm glad you qualified the age part, because it does make a difference. For instance, I would completely understand if your elderly parents were visiting and you simply said, "Oh! You can catch up on *Psych* on Netflix while you're here. It's streaming season one right now," and they just looked at you as though you were speaking in tongues.

But yes, of course, a thirty-something professional should not need a primer on how to operate any of these gizmos. I myself have a Tassimo coffeemaker. I love it. It loves me. But if anyone besides me tries to use it, there is a great deal of angst. ("I can't get the little light to come on." And really, "little" light?) Ditto the microwave. ("Where's the setting for partial thaw of cream-based entrees? I can't find it!") Blenders befuddle normally capable adults, what with their On and Off button. My advice: Show them how everything operates once; then, they're on their own. Hopefully you won't find your Ph.D. sister-in-law sticking the meat tongs into the toaster while it's on, but nothing would surprise me.

Question: No matter how many times I've asked one particular houseguest not to feed weird stuff like candy to my dog, he insists on doing it. He thinks it's a cute

***thing that bonds him to the dog. How do I approach
this without offending him?***

Try saying: "That chocolate bar will kill my dog. It will cost
about $2,300 for the emergency vet visit, blood test, X-rays,
exploratory surgery, and eventual cremation and delivery of
the remains. We good here?"

This brings up another sticky issue for houseguests. We
have two cats these days, and I've had as many as five back
when I was a single woman who lived alone and subscribed to
Offensive Stereotypes Monthly. If you have a new houseguest,
be sure to let them know you have cats. You'd be surprised to
find out how many people are quite violently allergic to cats
and just how hard it is to understand them when they're all
blue in the face and choking to death. They're really dreadful
conversationalists when this happens.

***Question: My in-laws, who live out of state and visit
several times a year, hate to eat anywhere except
chain restaurants. We'd love to show them the wonderful little bistros in town, but they only want to go to
Red Lobster or T.G.I. Friday's and the like. What do
you make of this?***

Have you *had* the garlic cheese biscuits at Red Lobster? I
mean, there could be worse things than being forced to make
a meal on those babies, am I right?

I get that you want to show off your town and introduce your in-laws to the finer things, but really, it's completely out of their comfort zone and you may have to respect that.

My Aunt Verlie (yes, the one who makes bedroom shoes out of maxi pads decorated with little satin roses) is convinced that everyone should eat only at chain restaurants because these little intimate local spots you mentioned use fresh food instead of frozen, and, well, that shit will kill you.

Don't die on this hill. You can hit the bistros after they're gone. And by the way, your in-laws don't want to suffer through yet another lecture on the relative merits of the Chilean varietals to the perky little Hungarian red you just discovered. In fact, no one does.

Question: I can't prove it, but I'm 99 percent certain that my mother-in-law is snooping through our medicine cabinets when she visits. Should I say something to her about this?

I'm 100 percent certain that you should not. Of course your mother-in-law is going through your medicine cabinet. They all do it. Believe me, it's punishment enough for her to know that you use a testosterone supplement and you're only thirty-two and she can't talk about it with her daughter, because that would confirm that she snooped. Years ago, advice maven Ann Landers reprinted a reader's suggestion to fill the medicine cabinet with marbles to find out who is snooping. This way, when the offender opened the door, the marbles would noisily spill out and the perp would be exposed. While this would be fun for about twenty seconds, it wouldn't be worth it in the long run. Keep the peace: When Mom visits, remove anything controversial from the medicine cabinet and put it in your sock drawer. The locked one where you keep your porn. You're welcome.

Question: This is rather indelicate, but I simply must ask—is it poor etiquette for my boyfriend and me to have sex in a guest bedroom while visiting relatives who have invited us to D.C.? No one seems to mind that we sleep together, and, well, we are normal, healthy adults. Shouldn't they expect that we would "enjoy ourselves" on vacation?

Oh, that's just gross. Your relatives are opening their home to you so you'll have a free place to stay while you spend the day visiting the Smithsonian, the U.S. Treasury, the Washington Monument, the Lincoln Memorial, and myriad other must-see spots in our nation's capital. What they are not doing is offering you a place to do the devil's aerobics like a couple of hormonally charged teenagers let loose in Cabo.

Just so you realize that, yes, I do understand the throes of passion and the time-honored appeal of doing it where you hadn't oughta, I suppose it's not so completely terrible as long as you promise to very discreetly launder your sheets, therefore not subjecting your hosts to the odious chore of dealing with a veritable palette of your bodily fluids.

I'm fairly certain you're sticking your lower lip out now in your best approximation of a pout. As Aunt Verlie might put it: "You can walk all the way to Grant's Tomb on that lip."

chapter 27

A Christmas Story

To understand how I set my hair on fire while decorating the Christmas tree, we need to start at the beginning. As always, we'd driven out to the country to fetch our cedar tree. Duh Hubby's family always has cedars because they love the challenge of trying to find tree ornaments that weigh less than a coffee filter.

We found the perfect tree quickly. Duh fired up the chain saw, and the Princess and I once again celebrated the Annual Narrow Miss of What Appears to Be an Important Leg Artery. As usual, we forgot the twine so we tied the cedar tree to the roof of the car with an extension cord and jumper cables. McDuhver!

We also tied it with the tree trunk facing the rear because Duh believes that if you drive 70 mph on the interstate back home as we did, a sturdy headwind is the best way to "get rid of all the loose needles." Also 60 percent of the tree, but who am I to quibble with physics?

At home we relived the tradition of putting the tree into the Stand That Never Works, somehow wedging an eight-foot-tall tree into a stand we bought from Dollar General twelve years ago and anchoring it to the floor with just the right mix of hardback books. It's a vision.

To further secure the tree, Duh employed his patented technique of screwing fishing line into the windowsill and then tying it to either side of the tree. Ornaments were administered, cider was sipped, Nat King Cole crooned. Even the Elf on the Shelf seemed happy from his judgmental little perch on the mantel.

Things were going well until I placed the very last ornament on the front of the tree, which, apparently mortified by all it had endured, suddenly pitched forward into the fireplace.

This is still not how I caught my hair on fire.

The Princess squealed as glass ornaments went flying. I suggested she put her shoes on while we cleaned up the shards, but she said she didn't know where they were.

While Duh and the Princess held the tree upright, I lay on the floor and tried to place the screws from the stand into the trunk again. It took a long time. So long, I didn't notice the huge tangled ball of lights over my head.

"What's that smell?" asked Duh.

"Ha ha!" said the Princess. "Mommy's hair's on fire!"

I beat at my head with my hands, which just made them laugh harder.

"Whatever you do, don't take the screws all the way out of the stand," said Duh, moments later. "You can never get them back in again."

I looked at him crazily from beneath singed bangs. "You mean like *this*?"

Duh looked at me like I was holding a grenade pin.

The next day, with the tree still lying pitifully on the living room floor, but oddly anchored by fishing line like a cedar Gulliver, I bought the mack daddy of Christmas tree stands.

"Whoa," said the saleswoman. "We don't sell many of these. Do you own a mall or something?"

Funny.

A Word About RSVP's

Ahhh, Christmas. The most wonderful time for a beer. I don't want to sound like a Grinch about it, but the holidays can challenge even the most well-mannered among us. Let's start with the opening salvo of the season: the holiday party.

You work for weeks ahead, polishing the silver, ironing the linens, and tinkering with the menu until it is perfect. You mail clever invitations that convey a sense of refined merriment. At the bottom right corner, there are four little letters that will be completely ignored by most of your invitees: RSVP.

These letters stand for *respondez s'il vous plait,* which is French for "please respond."

I have no idea why we live in the United States of America and continue to use this French abbreviation, but I guess, like peeing in the shower, it has just become a habit. Okay, maybe not exactly like that, but you get the idea.

Please, if you learn nothing else from reading this book, resolve here and now never to ignore the RSVP. (You must do this for *all* parties and events, including and especially weddings. It truly is what separates us from the savages.) For heaven's sake, your hosts aren't asking you to donate your corneas; they're asking you to call, text, or even e-mail a response so they'll know whether or not you're coming. (If the invitation specifies "regrets only," it means just that: You need only respond if you don't intend to go.) This simple act will take you about thirty-five seconds and will help them immensely in planning for food and beverages. Is it really that hard? We hear you: "I forgot" or "They know we're coming; we always come" or "They know I'm an inconsiderate loser and they should know that I'm never going to actually respond. But I plan to be there. I think. Unless something better comes along. Which it could. I'll let you know."

I hear this from hosts all the time. Some of them are so irritated (and I don't blame them a bit) that they form a sort of last-minute phone bank to call everyone on the list and ask them for a yes or no. Really, if you're spending hundreds on booze and food, should you have to treat your guests like they're tiny children?

Can you tell how much this particular etiquette violation pisses me off? *Can you???*

As if this situation isn't troubling enough, we really have trouble understanding people who won't even respond to an "e-vite." There it all is, on a screen right in front of you. All you have to do is click Yes or No. And you just can't do it, can you? There's even a Maybe option for folks who might have to work that day or just aren't sure yet. We can always come back to the maybes for confirmation.

I know this is rude, but I can't help but think that it would be fitting punishment to seat the folks who show up at your lovely party despite having not RSVP'd in the kitchen. Place an empty bowl and a box of Rice Krispies in front of them and say, "Have at it. We'll be in the other room, enjoying a sumptuous prime rib, sautéed asparagus, and those cool little puffed potato thingies that I've been working on *for three frickin' days.* Bon appétit!"

Question: The other day I overheard one of my neighbors snickering about the Christmas letter that I send out every year to friends and family. Frankly, I was hurt. I spend a lot of time and effort updating everyone on our family's "happenings." Should I continue

to send the letter, or is it really just something that people make fun of?

The answer is yes to both your questions. You shouldn't stop sending the single best source of a genuine belly laugh that many of us get all year long. It would be incredibly rude of you to just cut us off without warning. How will we ever go an entire year without an update on your oldest son's stratospheric GPA. You actually wrote last year: "Will it be Harvard? Will it be Yale? The world is his oyster!" And your precious daughter, the ballerina? Did she win the role of Sugarplum Fairy this year in *The Nutcracker* again? Don't leave us hanging!

So much fun has been poked at the Christmas letter that I've noticed some senders seem to be toning down the bragging and even poking a little fun at themselves. I just hate that. Even the distant cousin who one year bragged of "finally getting approved for a Visa platinum card so suckit CreditReport.Com!" has shaped up and, in the most recent letter, wrote of dissatisfaction at work and mild regret at having put her baby daughter in the pageant circuit—a rollercoaster ride of expensive costumes, sparkly cowgirl hats, flippers, extensions, tanning, and Red Bull. "Still and all," she wrote, "when I saw the look on her little nine-month-old face when she won the Sparkle Baby title, it was all worth it. . . ." Yes!

Question: What's the proper etiquette on Christmas cards? In other words, is it okay to drop someone from the list if you've sent them a card for five years and they've never reciprocated?

That depends. It's possible that, through their lack of response, they're telling you that (a) they don't do cards, and (b) even if they did, they probably wouldn't send one to you. That said, you should really consider your own motives in sending these cards. If you are sending them to people you genuinely care about, then it shouldn't matter that they aren't "card people." Some people enjoy receiving them, but they are just never going to reciprocate because they're lazy, unmotivated, cheap, or all three.

The point is, their bad behavior or disinterest shouldn't dissuade you from sending them a card if you genuinely like them and want to send a traditional greeting that shows you're thinking of them. Take the high road and keep sending them if your motives are pure. If you're just hoping for reciprocity so you can finally have enough cards to decorate that archway in the den, well, you might want to rethink the whole card thing.

Question: I hate sounding ungrateful, but my friend gives the weirdest Christmas presents. It's almost always something from a resale store. Is it too much to

ask for a present to be something that no one else has ever worn before?

No, it's not, but this is a test of how well-mannered you can be under extraordinarily awful circumstances. We all know people who love the planet so mightily that they insist on giving recycled gifts even as they speed away in their shiny new cars. Hmmm.

Because Duh's family is just about the dearest bunch of folks there is, some insist on giving only handmade gifts or perhaps a poem they have written especially for each family member. It's a maddeningly lovely tradition that leaves me wondering if they are all so directionally challenged that they can't find the local mall with both hands and a flashlight. I mean homemade stuff is cute if you're Laura Ingalls and the mall is, like, one hundred years away, but haven't we progressed to the point of buying mass-produced goods from China in delightfully flattering colors and styles? Do I hear an "amen"?

Oops. Did I just write that out loud? The proper reaction to these "gifts from the (blech) heart" should be one of appreciation. Fake it till you make it. I think I once heard a roomful of alcoholics say that.

Question: While we're on the subject of gift-giving, is it okay to leave the price tag on so the recipient

will know that you really spent a lot of money on them?

I'm sorry. Is there anyone out there who's not a complete and total asshole who has a question for me?

Question: Our office holiday party got a little out of hand, and I drunkenly kissed my married boss. Things are going to be awkward now. What should I do?

You're killing me, here. Really, anyone at all?

Question: My daughter's little friend, who is also eight, just told her that Santa isn't real. I want to march right over to that kid's house and give her a piece of my mind. What's the right thing to do?

Okay, you honestly expect me to endorse a plan in which you arrive on an eight-year-old's doorstep screeching at her because she told your kid the truth? I hate to break it to you, but your kid's not all that bright or she would've never told you this. The Princess knew that Santa wasn't real for years. Finally, when she was about twelve and we were "leaving cookies for Santa and Rudolph," the Princess admitted that she'd known about Santa for years but was afraid that if she told us, she'd get fewer presents. That's how most kids do it. Now, calm your spiteful ass down.

The Last Word

Nobody's perfect. No sooner had I finished this book than I realized I'd forgotten to RSVP for a neighborhood party; found myself using my fingers to coax some rice onto a fork (mercifully in the privacy of my own bathroom; okay, that may be a twofer violation); and, worst of all, flat-out forgot to write a proper thank-you note to a friend who nominated me for a fancy award I didn't really deserve.

We're suffocatingly busy sometimes—okay, all the time—and it's hard to find the time for the niceties. But we must. While I would love for the Princess to be able to identify the fish fork (mostly so she can tell me which one it is), I'm much more concerned that she treat others with kindness and tenderness. That's the essence of all this manners business: the care of those around you, whether friend or stranger. At its heart and soul, etiquette is all about putting others at ease, whether that's through a well-earned compliment or an engaging conversation in which you actually listen to what someone is saying rather than planning your response while they're talking. Hard to do, I know.

But let's try, shall we?

And if there's an etiquette question that is causing you concern and wasn't addressed in these pages, please feel free to shoot me an e-mail (or if you really want to suck up, a handwritten note on engraved stationery), and we'll discuss. Politely, of course.

Celia Rivenbark
Wilmington, North Carolina